LESSONS & LACE

LESSONS & LACE

Everything I Know
About Dreams, Heartbreak,
and Magic
I Learned from
Stevie Nicks

RACHEL BRODSKY

HARMONY
NEW YORK

Harmony Books
An imprint of Random House
A division of Penguin Random House LLC
1745 Broadway, New York, NY 10019
harmonybooks.com | randomhousebooks.com
penguinrandomhouse.com

Library of Congress Cataloging-in-Publication Data

ISBN 9780593981061
Ebook ISBN 9780593981078

Printed in China

2 4 6 8 9 7 5 3 1

FIRST EDITION

BOOK TEAM: Production editor: Dennis Ambrose • Managing editor: Allison Fox • Production manager: Kevin Garcia • Copy editor: Emily DeHuff • Proofreaders: Claire Maby, Melissa Churchill, Caryl Schwartz

Book design by Elizabeth Rendfleisch

Illustrations: Niall Grant
Lace art: Sveta_Aho/Adobe Stock

The authorized representative in the EU for product safety and compliance is Penguin Random House Ireland, Morrison Chambers, 32 Nassau Street, Dublin D02 YH68, Ireland. https://eu-contact.penguin.ie

For my dad

CONTENTS

INTRODUCTION

WELCOME TO THE CHURCH OF STEVIE

I'd like to be remembered as a notoriously eclectic person: a collector and a dancer and a singer and a songwriter and a fairy-dust spreader.

—Stevie Nicks, Us magazine, 1990

I'd like to begin with a confession: I had a slight obsession with witches growing up. I'm qualifying this admission with the word "slight" because I never tried to learn any actual witchcraft, I never collected crystals or spellbooks, I wasn't wild about nature or the movie *Practical Magic* (the part where they bring Nicole Kidman's abusive boyfriend back to life scared me), and I can't say that I genuinely believed in magic or much else supernatural.

What really got me, though, were stories about women whom society had somehow deemed "different." Spin me a yarn about some punk rock lady who lived life according to her terms in any respect or time, and I was sold.

These women didn't have to resemble a classic Halloweeny witch—although sometimes they did. Like, what nineties kid didn't want to be Sarah Jessica Parker in *Hocus Pocus*? The ladies I looked up to included Disney heroines, Sabrina the Teenage Witch, a Spice Girl or two, Harriet the Spy, Claudia Kincaid from *The Mixed-Up Files of Mrs. Basil E. Frankweiler*. The through line was that these girls went on adventures, they were hungry, they were ambitious, they wanted things they could not yet name. Most of the time, the "witch" stamp turned out to be a catchall for anyone who thought or behaved a little differently.

Witches had a funny way of showing up repeatedly in my

childhood. When I turned ten, my family moved mid-school-year to New Jersey, making me the new kid in class. On my first day, my new classmates pointed out another girl in our class, instructing me not to approach her. Why? Because apparently, she'd gone around telling everyone she was a witch. Of course, this only made her more interesting to me. Guess who my new BFF was after that?

My new witch friend and I quickly bonded over music and fashion, writing down all the different clothing items we'd buy if we could afford them: ball-chain necklaces, sprawling UFO pants, sky-high platforms, all-black everything. (It was the nineties.) When I asked her if she had in fact told everyone she was a witch, my friend admitted that she had, but only one time, just for kicks. (Amazing how the worst stuff sticks to you in childhood.) To me, this girl wasn't remotely scary or even particularly weird—she just had great taste. When the school year ended, we lost touch—our township was so big, it was always building new schools and shuffling kids around—but I like to think that my fifth grade friend went on to do exciting, witchy things befitting of her top-tier tastes.

The reason I'm telling you about my childhood witch craze is that, over the course of writing this book about pop music's wisdom-dispensing, moon-pendant-wearing godmother witch Stevie Nicks, I realized a few things. I realized how deeply I identified with reports from Stevie's childhood, when young Teedee (as she called herself) spent a lot of time indoors surrounded by her favorite records and storybooks full of fairy tales and folklore. I traced a line from my early obsession with "out there" personalities to my lifelong need to live completely, utterly on my own terms, and how, at certain points, I've felt pressured to defend my choices, whether it was leaving a toxic job prematurely, saying no when necessary, building my life in a way that felt authentic, or asking for more and better in my romantic relationships. And I learned *so much* from doing these things. Ultimately, and I think Stevie would agree with me, one of the hardest things you'll ever do is be brave enough to live in a way that feels authentic to you.

Anyway, I'd love to tell you that I grew up identifying with Stevie Nicks from the jump, but that wouldn't be entirely true. Instead, I discovered resonances with Stevie's singular journey over the course of my own life.

At first, there was music. Thanks to my parents, who were children of the seventies, I knew every Fleetwood Mac hit on classic rock radio by heart. The long-running British-American blues-turned-pop/rock collective was a staple in our house, along with other marquee names of the era: Tom Petty, the Eagles, the Who, the Allman Brothers, the Rolling Stones, Crosby, Stills, Nash & Young, Creedence, Carole King, the Carpenters, Simon & Garfunkel. Fleetwood Mac bridged the gap between my parents' individual car radio station choices; songs like "Dreams" and "Rhiannon" showed up on my dad's preferred classic rock stations just as frequently as on my mom's soft rock / adult contemporary airwaves.

Anyway, this is all to say that my generation considers Fleetwood Mac and Stevie Nicks's solo material foundational to any worthy pop music education, right up there with the Beatles, Tom Petty, and David Bowie. This was the music playing in the background anywhere we went—on the car radio, at the mall, at the movies, in the local diner. Classic rock/pop's ubiquity could make it easy to take for granted, to forget what these artists did to move the cultural needle.

This particularly applies to Stevie Nicks. Today widely recognized as a contemporary pop music icon and beloved mentor, Stevie was once underestimated, misunderstood, dismissed, and mocked by her peers, industry, and critics. (Not to mention repeatedly called a witch.)

We tend to gloss over everything Stevie had to endure to come out on the other side as rock's patron saint of lessons learned. We lose sight of the blatantly sexist interviews that framed her as a boy-crazy space cadet, a flighty and unserious writer of overwrought romance. Not unlike how, in the 1994 film adaptation of *Little Women,* Jo March is told by a publisher to "try one of the ladies' magazines" for her "sentiment and fairy stories."

It may not be the 1970s anymore, but I would argue that it's still a little dicey for an unapologetic romantic who chases happiness—or really for any person containing multitudes. A much more recent example mirroring Stevie's early experience is Taylor Swift, another songwriting icon who has drawn enormous influence from Stevie. For the first decade or so of Taylor's career, she was unilaterally dismissed as boy-crazy, unserious, and unnecessarily vengeful in her songwriting.

Society may have changed, gender discussions may have evolved, and popular media might be more empathetic as it interviews famous women, but it's still an alienating experience to be perceived as one or more of these things: different, independent, happiness-chasing, childfree, selfish, ambitious, creative, brave. (Or witch. Potato, po-*tah*-to.)

Today, Stevie Nicks has definitively made it to the other side of nearly every public obstacle she has ever faced. She got herself to Hollywood, she helped popularize a floundering midlevel rock band, she got out from under the shadow of her first creative partner, she proved her viability as a commercially successful solo act, she beat addiction, she got healthy . . . and she just kept going, becoming a friend, mentor, and spiritual guiding light to her fellow songwriters, generations of fans, and goodness knows how many godchildren. She has become a uniquely down-to-earth, tell-it-straight paragon of truth telling and self-actualization. But she didn't get here without taking a lot of hard looks in the mirror.

Within this book, you'll read about Stevie's remarkable life and music through the lens of lessons and wisdom—all of which she gained by facing certain challenges head-on. I pored over years' worth of archival interviews in magazines and books, news programs, documentaries, song lyrics, and insights from people who've spent ample time in Stevie's orbit. I hope what emerges is a portrait of a woman and prolific writer who values emotional and artistic growth, vulnerability and quiet introspection, romantic love and sisterhood, freedom of expression, relatability, spirituality, career ambition, and, above all, the space to honestly and authentically be herself.

My genuine hope is that by immersing yourself in Stevie's life and lessons, you, too, will be inspired, in whatever way resonates, to embrace your own wild heart. To say the thing you're scared to say. To create something beautiful, whether you share it with others or not. But if you take anything from this book, just know that it can be summarized in one clairvoyant sentence, which Stevie wrote in a letter as the world descended into the global COVID-19 lockdown. It might be specific to the year 2020, but it also applies to just about anything:

Just Dance. This will pass. Love will find a way. It always does.

LESSONS & LACE

QUEEN OF SWORDS
QUEEN OF WANDS

LESSON ONE

BELIEVE IN DESTINY

I came here for a reason. I didn't come here to be a mother. I didn't come here to be a nun. And I did not come here to be a cleaning lady. I came here to be a poet.

—Stevie Nicks, Rolling Stone, 2002

If you believe in destiny—which I do—it seems like my life was pretty mapped out. It seems almost like there was somebody up there moving the chess [pieces]. And I was the white queen, and I just went where I was moved....

—Stevie Nicks, Us magazine, 1990

In 2014, the original lineup of Fleetwood Mac reunited for their On with the Show tour. I got my credit card out and forked over much more than I would typically pay for two nosebleed seats at Madison Square Garden. I called my dad, the obvious plus one for this event, and told him to save the date.

The night we saw Fleetwood Mac, I checked my email and saw a message from the senior editor of *SPIN* magazine, where I'd just applied to an opening, inviting me to interview. I was beside myself with joy—here I was watching Fleetwood Mac with my dad (their biggest fan) and reading a life-changing work email. That very week, I secured the job. My professional life would never be the same. Was it destiny? The romantic in me likes to think that it was.

Stevie Nicks has long believed in *her* destiny. Years before she possessed the words or self-awareness to say *This will be my path in life,* all Stevie had was a persistent feeling that she was meant to sing, write, and perform. Half a century of pop music history has confirmed her premonitions. But what were Stevie's first steps toward realizing her destiny?

Stephanie Lynn Nicks was born on May 26, 1948, at Good Samaritan Hospital in Phoenix, Arizona. Her parents, Barbara

Meeks-Nicks and Aaron Jess Seth Nicks, Jr., had been college sweethearts at Arizona State University and were married in 1947. "When I met Jess, I wrote in my diary that this was the man I was going to marry," said Barbara, describing the moment they met as "love at first sight."

The older of their two children (Stevie's younger brother, Christopher, was born in 1953), Stevie got her now permanent nickname after mispronouncing "Stephanie" as "Teedee" as a little girl. After that, Barbara liked to refer to her daughter as Teedee as a term of endearment.

Even before she was old enough to form words, Stevie felt magnetized to music. Her responses were visceral. When she was a baby, Stevie's parents would play her music because she seemed to respond so favorably to it. "My mom said that I started singing when I was very young," Stevie remembered in 1992. "They always had music going for me because I seemed to have such a love for it. Even as a baby in a crib, I wanted music."

Meanwhile, Stevie's paternal grandfather, Aaron "A.J." Nicks, had been a country and western performer in Arizona and strongly encouraged his granddaughter's budding interest. In fact, Stevie's first live performance was with her grandfather; the two sang a duet version of Red Sovine's "Are You Mine?"

"My dad's father . . . brought music into my life as soon as I was able to understand music at all," Stevie said. "I was singing duets with my grandfather when I was four. My grandfather rode the railway trains across the country and played in different places. He played harmonica, fiddle, and guitar. He wasn't a great musician, but he was a really good songwriter. I'm kind of the same way. I consider myself a good songwriter, but I'm not a very good musician."

A.J. Nicks also taught Stevie how to sing harmony (something she'd go on to become famous for in Fleetwood Mac and after), calling her a "perfect Everly Brother" and urging her to "put [her] heart into it." Their outings got a little bigger when Stevie turned five—A.J. would take their grandfather-granddaughter act on the road to the local saloons, where patrons would cheer for Stevie, who'd dance on the bar counters in a little cowgirl outfit. For her trouble, A.J. paid Stevie fifty cents a pop.

"When she was about four or five years old, her granddad made her a tiny little guitar," Jess told *Arizona Living* in 1983. "From that point forward, she showed an aptitude and a desire to be involved in music. We gave her lessons, mainly on the guitar, and when she was old enough, we bought her a very good classical guitar. She was always extroverted. She loved to perform, loved to sing and loved to write songs."

When Stevie's family briefly lived in Los Angeles, they opened a Mexican-style bar, where Barbara would cook and the men in the family would hang out and sing together, much to Stevie's delight. "I can remember being there at about two in the afternoon. . . . No one [else was] really in there . . . I remember singing with my granddad and feeling even at that young age that music was definitely going to be a part of my life."

Stevie and A.J.'s granddad-granddaughter act never got very far; Barbara balked at A.J.'s request to take Stevie out of town to perform, and an angry A.J. reportedly didn't speak to the family for two years after that. But Barbara had her reasons for not letting Stevie go on the road with A.J., who was not exactly the picture of stability. Even as Stevie got older, her parents were supportive of her creative aspirations but urged her to proceed with caution, lest she spend her adulthood aimlessly hopping trains, forever in search of the next paid gig. "My granddad . . . left his family and took freight trains and traveled all over, playing in bars and supporting himself by playing pool," Stevie later said. "So my mom and dad thought, well, there she goes. She's gonna walk down the same road as her grandfather. Luckily, I became a bit more successful than he was."

Stevie's father, Jess, also led a markedly different life than his transient musician dad. An aspiring corporate executive, Jess moved up quickly in the business world, holding major positions with Lucky Lager Brewing Company in San Francisco, Armour & Co., and eventually Greyhound. As a result of her father's work, Stevie and her family were constantly moving to different cities. Over the years, they lived in Los Angeles, Albuquerque, El Paso, Chicago, Salt Lake City, back to Los Angeles, and San Francisco.

Moving around that much would be destabilizing for just

about any little kid, but Stevie adapted by realizing that sociability meant survival. "In my life we moved so much that I was always the new girl, and if you are the new girl, you better have some social skills," she once said.

Stevie also found an anchor in the pop and folk music of the day. Listening to early-sixties hits by the Supremes, the Shirelles, and the Chiffons, Stevie started noticing and studying song structure—to the point where she once shushed her parents, who were talking over the radio, so she could concentrate on how the song fitted together.

"In the beginning, there was a song," she said while accepting the BMI Songwriting Award in 2014. "I was in the fourth grade and lived in El Paso, Texas. I heard it on the radio, bought it, and learned it. Then me and two of my little friends performed and sang for anyone and everyone that would listen. It was called 'You Cheated (You Lied).' . . . I fell in love with it."

"I have been a little performer since I was four years old . . . I was just nuts for the stage," Stevie also remembered in 2012. "I came into the world dancing and singing, and my mom and dad, I think, knew from the very beginning . . . My parents were very supportive of my love of music, and my focus was very strong from when I was in grade school. They knew I didn't want to be an actress, I didn't want to take drama, I didn't really want to take musical drama. I just wanted to listen to rockabilly and rock 'n' roll and R&B, and I just was in my own little musical world. . . . In sixth grade, I was wearing a black outfit with a top hat. I had it all planned out."

That doo-wop song would be one of many radio hits inspiring Stevie, who felt equally drawn to popular singles from the pioneering rock 'n' roller Buddy Holly. "I think me and the same friends did a tap dance in a talent show [in sixth grade to] 'Everyday.'"

Early accounts of Stevie's life also recall her mother, a devout Catholic and homemaker, as protective. Though Barbara let Stevie take dance and drama lessons, she preferred her daughter not to spend too much time outside the family house. As a result of spending so much time on her own, Stevie let her mind wander to stories, fantasies, fairy tales, and folklore. "She says today that she still spends a lot of time alone," the rock biographer Stephen Davis told *Interview* magazine. "She does her best writing when she's alone and she's sort of used to it. It's a typical writer or artist's upbringing, but surprising in the context of someone who became a rock star."

When school let out, Stevie spent summers in Ajo, Arizona, with Barbara's mother, Grandma Alice Harwood (Crazy Alice, as the family tended to call her, on account of her eccentricities), who sang lullabies and read books out loud to her.

After A.J. fell out with Barbara and Jess, he disappeared to Bozeman, Montana, and then Winona, Minnesota. Eventually, he resurfaced in El Paso, Texas, when Stevie was in the fourth grade, and the two got their chance to reconnect. A.J. bought his granddaughter 45s by the Everly Brothers and got her singing harmony again, this time to "It's Late" by Dorsey Burnette.

In the late 1950s, the Nicks family relocated again, to the vastly more conservative Salt Lake City, where doing the Twist was discouraged in favor of more wholesome activities like baton twirling, which Stevie did when she wasn't listening to the radio (and would do again in the Fleetwood Mac video for "Tusk"), taking dance lessons, singing in a cappella groups, and writing in her journal. She was a popular student in Salt Lake City, where she won a prize for tap dancing in a black top hat at the school talent show.

As Stevie came of age, Jess and Barbara continued to encourage her interest in music, though always with the caveat that if this was going to be her life path, then she should also approach it with a healthy dose of pragmatism. "I was so heavily into music that they gave up," Stevie later told *High Times.* "I mean, they knew I was on my way to something. The only thing my dad ever said to me was—because my dad was very successful and very ambitious—'If you're going to do this, you better be the very best.' That was the only thing he ever said to me. 'I don't want to see you being second.'" No pressure, right? But what else could you really expect from a corporate executive vice president?

"That was a pretty heavy thing to say to me," Stevie continued before relenting: "He strives to get the best out of me, and you don't get the best out of me by hugging and kissing me and telling me how wonderful I am. That doesn't work. The best thing to do is really be serious with me and I'll work hard."

In 1963, Stevie's family relocated yet again, from Salt Lake City to Arcadia, California, about thirteen miles northeast of Los Angeles. "[We lived] right across the street from the Santa Anita racetrack—pretty ritzy in comparison to Salt Lake," Stevie later recalled of this time. While attending Arcadia High School, Stevie met her soon-to-be best friend Robin Snyder, who would eventually travel around the world as Stevie's vocal coach (among other duties) in Fleetwood Mac. Also at Arcadia, Stevie sang in a moderately popular folk trio called Changing Times (named for Bob Dylan, naturally) from 1964 to 1965.

When Stevie was fifteen, Jess Nicks arranged through a contact at Twentieth Century Fox in Los Angeles for Stevie to audition with the record producer Jackie Mills, a former jazz drummer turned producer for Capitol Records. She wound up signing a five-year contract, though it's unclear precisely with whom she was signed. In his book *Mirror in the Sky,* the writer and music historian Simon Morrison guesses it might have been Liberty Records, where Mills worked in the early 1960s. Mills lost his job, however, in 1963; the label was sold, and Stevie's contract was annulled. Welcome to show business.

Then, for her sixteenth birthday, Stevie's parents gave their daughter six weeks of guitar lessons with a local musician who played in the classical Spanish style. Once the six weeks were up, the teacher announced plans to move to Seville, but Stevie was hooked. She begged her parents to buy her the small Goya parlor guitar from her lessons, which they did.

Not only did Stevie keep practicing on that guitar, she used it to write her very first original song: a breakup ballad called "I've Loved and I've Lost and I'm Sad but Not Blue" about a "really handsome boy" who'd pinballed back and forth between her and a girlfriend. "I was totally in tears sitting on my bed with lots of paper, my guitar, and a pen, and I wrote this song about your basic sixteen-year-old love affair thing," she later said. "When I played my own song that night, I knew [from] that second on that I was not going to do a lot of other people's songs. I had to write my own."

Later, she told *Interview* magazine that even as a teenager, "I absolutely knew I was gonna be famous. . . . I knew from when I first wrote my first song about the first love of my life, and sat there on my bed and watched myself play it in the mirror with tears running down my face. . . . I just knew that that was the only thing I could ever really do—write songs and sing them to people."

Even at sixteen, Stevie was laying the thematic groundwork for what would become her most famous breakup songs, particularly with Fleetwood Mac. Consider her perspective within a song title like "I've Loved and I've Lost"—yes, she's drowning in the pain of rejection and permitting herself to feel those feelings, but simultaneously there's a growing resolve and acknowledgment that the pain will be finite. A decade from then, Stevie would use songs like "Dreams," "Silver Springs," and "Landslide" to simultaneously express deep disappointment in a romantic outcome while hinting at resilience and self-love amid the mess.

In 1966, the Nicks family again relocated, this time to the San Francisco suburb of Menlo Park. Menlo-Atherton High was a preppy school where kids had their own cars (a big deal in the sixties) and families employed household help. During her senior year, Stevie participated in the High Spirits glee club and excelled in subjects like English and drama. Every now and then she'd pass in the halls a boy one year her junior named Lindsey Buckingham, a California-born and -raised guitar autodidact who grew up listening to Chuck Berry, Elvis, and the Everly Brothers.

"I met Lindsey at a religious meeting called 'the Young Life' that they used to have at high school," Stevie told *BAM* in 1981. "He was sitting there just gorgeous, playing his guitar, and I walked over to him, and we sang 'California Dreamin',' and we sang it perfect."

The two wouldn't start collaborating in earnest for a couple of years—romantically or creatively—but Stevie's interest was definitely piqued. "When I first met him, he was going with somebody and so was I, but I fell totally in love with him. I was captivated," she said. Lindsey didn't give much away, but she guessed he approved of her harmonizing to the

Mamas & the Papas because he started up another song with her right away.

Upon graduating from high school, Stevie didn't have any firm plans. Her parents pushed her to at least try some college, so Stevie enrolled at the College of San Mateo for two years and then, in 1968, transferred to San Jose State, where she majored in speech communication. She was also itching to start or join a band.

As fortune would have it, an old friend from high school, Bob Aguirre, called Stevie up wanting to know if she'd consider auditioning to sing in Fritz, a psych rock group he played drums in with Lindsey Buckingham, who was then on bass. Also featuring Brian Kane (guitar, vocals), Javier Pacheco (keys, vocals), Jody Moreing (bass), and Cal Roper (bass), "Fritz" had been shortened from "the Fritz Rabyne Memorial Band," which referenced a real person—a student the group knew in high school who was still very much alive. His pupils selected the name for their band at random, and they never knew what the real Fritz Rabyne thought of their tribute, since he moved away and lost touch before they could ask him. No matter—"the Fritz Rabyne Memorial Band" got shaved down to just "Fritz," and Stevie joined up without quite knowing what she was getting into.

Stevie's experience in Fritz was, in a word, complicated. On one hand, she finally had a space to play with other musicians and develop her live performance, which, up until then, mainly consisted of her strumming acoustic country ballads.

When I played my own song that night, I knew [from] that second on that I was not going to do a lot of other people's songs. I had to write my own.

At the same time, Stevie's male bandmates seemed irritated by her increasingly dynamic and theatrical stage persona. When she did her own charismatic version of the Stone Poneys' "Different Drum," fans went absolutely crazy. But Javier Pacheco was not impressed. He found Stevie's emotional performance style to be a "big put-on" and would tease her constantly. (Javier would later walk his criticism back, telling fans in an online Q&A that he'd been blinded by "silly machismo and arrogance.")

"Nobody in that band wanted me as their girlfriend because I was too ambitious for them," Stevie told *Rolling Stone* in 1977. "They all thought I was in it for the attention and didn't take me seriously at all. I was just a girl singer, and they hated the fact that I got a lot of the credit."

After playing local shows, like at the Stanford University quad, "within two or three months we were opening for Hendrix, Janis Joplin, all the San Francisco bands." Later, Stevie reflected on the ways her time in Fritz prepared her for what would become a massive career in pop and rock. "I could never figure out why I stayed in that band," she continued. "Now I know that was the preparation for Fleetwood Mac."

Singing in Fritz also built her confidence. "I knew that I was Stevie Nicks after about three weeks of being in Fritz," Stevie told *MOJO*. "I would stroll through San Jose State with my guitar case thinking, 'Does everybody know who I am? I'm a rock star.' I felt it and I believed it."

The venerated music venues Fritz started playing at bolstered her feeling of empowerment. Not only was the band performing at the Fillmore, Winterland, and the Avalon, but they were opening for and surrounded by some of the era's greatest rock innovators: Santana, Jefferson Airplane, Janis Joplin. Stevie drew tremendous inspiration from watching Grace Slick's "slinkiness" and Janis Joplin's full-bodied stage domination. "You couldn't have pried me away with a million-dollar check," she said. "I was glued to her. I said, 'If I ever am a performer of any value, I want to be able to create the same feeling that is going on between her and her audience.' Janis was tough but sang like a bird and could really hold the audience in her hand."

But it wasn't all love and light when Stevie crossed paths with Joplin for the first time. "When I first met Janis, she was very angry," Stevie told the *Telegraph* in 2011. "The first band had run over time, and she came on stage screaming, [it] scared me to death. I was hiding behind the camps. She told them to get the you-know-what off her you-know-what stage. And they wrapped it up!"

"Thirty minutes later," Stevie recalled in 2008, "on comes Janis, very different, feathers in her hair, fantastic bell bottoms, really high-heeled shoes, and a top with little bell sleeves in silky, beautiful material and beads and wild, crazy curly hair. I was blown away by her. I learned more from her during that hour and a half—watching how she dealt with the crowd, how she paced herself, how she sang—than any hour and a half in my life."

Fritz's prime opening slots soon netted them a manager, David Forest, who thought the group should consider relocating to Los Angeles. The prospect held very little interest for most of Fritz, who chafed at LA's "plastic" reputation and wanted to remain in the Bay Area, where art was taken seriously (albeit heavily monetized). Nonetheless, Forest called around and got LA producer Keith Olsen to come up and take in a Fritz show. Olsen's main takeaway was that Lindsey and Stevie had star power—had they ever thought about breaking off on their own?

As the sixties waned, Fritz began to fizzle. They recorded a little with Olsen at the Sound City studios in Van Nuys, but it was mostly just a formality, and nothing substantial ever came of it. Stevie and Lindsey had grown closer, however, and seemed to be on their own path. "I took Lindsey and Stevie aside and said to them, 'You two have a unique sound together . . . but the rest of your band will hold you back. I'd like to continue to work with you, but I think you'd do much better as a duo.'"

When the other Fritz members decided to leave LA for good, Stevie and Lindsey stayed behind and called their new act Buckingham Nicks. Olsen heartily believed in their potential to make it big, and for now, that would have to be enough.

HOLLYWOOD

LESSON TWO

GO FEARLESSLY INTO THE DARK

So many of these songs [on Buckingham Nicks] are about me and Lindsey moving to LA in 1971, asking each other, "Now what? Should we go back to San Francisco? Should we quit?" We were scared kids in this big, huge, flat city where we had no friends and no money.

—Stevie Nicks, Rolling Stone, 2014

I am pretty fearless, and you know why? Because I don't handle fear very well; I'm not a good terrified person. I learned that a long time ago. You know when you walk into your house and there's nobody there and all the lights are out, it's like I just fearlessly go into the dark, because I know if I start creepin' out that it'll get me. So I just try not to ever be afraid of anything. I just go, "Well, if the earthquake happens, I've got my steel-toed shoes and some rope, and we'll get down a mountain." Or you'll be up there in a helicopter waving at us. I believe that we will just about get through anything.

—Stevie Nicks, Interview magazine, 2001

Stevie and Lindsey had decided to stick around Los Angeles and move in with Keith Olsen. Stevie's parents, while supportive in theory, remained skeptical that their eldest would secure that pie-in-the-sky rock star dream. Quit school to live with a boy in LA? At a near-stranger's house? "'What are you gonna do?' [my parents asked.] 'Be in the circus for the rest of your life?'"

If the music industry was a circus, Stevie had already run away to join. She wasn't a featured act yet. All she had were her notebooks, a few dollars, her Goya guitar, and endless dreams. If LA was where she needed to be to chase them down, then that's where she'd have to be.

Shacking up at Olsen's house off Coldwater Canyon Boulevard, Stevie and Lindsey threw themselves into songwriting, recording a demo tape of seven songs at Sound City. But record companies were slow to invest in the fledgling Buckingham Nicks, and the little family inheritance the duo moved to LA with was rapidly drying up. A year or so prior, Lindsey had received a little over ten thousand dollars from an aunt, which he partially used to buy a four-track tape machine. Lindsey was spending most of his time at Sound City (where the duo met a young assistant engineer named Richard Dashut; soon, the trio pooled their money for a place together in North Hollywood). Stevie picked up a series of odd jobs cleaning houses and waiting tables. Extra money from Mom and Dad wasn't really an option, as Cameron Crowe wrote when he profiled Fleetwood Mac for *Rolling Stone*. "I'd get money from them here and there," Stevie said. "But if I wanted to go back to school, if I wanted to move back home, then they would support me. . . . If I was gonna be here in LA doing my trip, I was gonna have to do it on my own."

Stevie would always sound matter-of-fact about this division of labor in interviews—after all, *someone* had to make rent if they were going to remain in Los Angeles, and Lindsey had flatly refused to perform around the local bar scene, which would have brought in semi-consistent cash. "I would have gone for that in a big way, personally, because singing in horrible places like those four hours a night is a helluva lot better than being a cleaning lady," Stevie later said in 1981. "That was the only real rift we had then. He won. But I loved him. I loved our music, and I was willing to do anything I could to get us to point B from point A."

"I didn't want to be a waitress, but I believed that Lindsey didn't have to work, that he should just lay on the floor and practice his guitar and become more brilliant every day," Stevie also told *SPIN* in 1997 about this time. "And as I watched him become more brilliant every day, I felt very gratified. I was totally devoted to making it happen for him. I never worried about not being successful; I wanted to make it possible for him to be successful. And when you feel that way about somebody, it's very easy to take your own personality and quiet it way down. I knew my career was going to work out fine. I knew I wasn't going to lose myself."

Meanwhile, in other interviews, Stevie veered into resentment of their arrangement, which conveniently placed Lindsey in social circles with other musicians while she cleaned houses and bused tables. "We were broke and starving," she told *Rolling Stone*. "I was cleaning the house of our producer for fifty dollars a week. I came home with my big Hoover vacuum cleaner, my Ajax, my toilet brush, my cleaning shoes on. And Lindsey had managed to have some idiot send him eleven ounces of opiated hash. He and all his friends are in a circle on the floor. They'd been smoking hash for a month, and I don't smoke because of my voice. I'd come home every day and have to step over these bodies. I'm tired, and I'm lifting their legs up so I can clean up and empty the ashtrays. And all these guys are going, 'I don't know why I don't feel very good.' I said, 'You want to know why you don't feel so good? I'll tell you why—because you've done nothing else for weeks but lie on my floor and smoke hash and take my money!'"

In 1973, the clouds finally parted. Buckingham Nicks was offered a deal with Polydor Records, which came with a recording budget of $25K and a chance to tour. Stevie immediately quit her gig at Bob's Big Boy and wrote letters to her parents telling them all about the big studio names coming to play on her and Lindsey's album, like drummer Jim Keltner and bassist Jerry Scheff, who'd previously played with Elvis and the Doors.

"Well, here I am—once again at the 'famous' Sound City Recording Studio," Stevie wrote in a letter to her family as she and Lindsey recorded their debut. "I am getting very tired of sitting around listening to twelve hours of music per day. Oh well, I know it will pay off in the end, and when I am sitting in my small but luxurious Beverly Hills home overlooking my small but tasteful pool that is totally secluded, where I can sun in the nude and tan my entire fat body while waiting for my plastic surgery leg lift—it will all be worth it. Otherwise, everything here is just 'peach-y.'"

But getting Buckingham Nicks's debut (and only) album off the ground was stressful for Stevie, whom studio guitarist and longtime friend Waddy Wachtel remembered as "still very innocent at that point. She was like this little folksinger girl." Stevie walked away feeling embarrassed by the album's cover: a black-and-white image of her and Lindsey without their shirts. Stevie had gone into the photo shoot—taking place at Lorrie Sullivan's Burbank studio—wearing a loose-fitting white blouse. It had been a splurge, costing $111 (about $786 today). Sullivan, who was working with the photographer Jimmy Wachtel (Waddy's brother), was under instruction from Polydor to lean into the couple's sex appeal. When Jimmy asked her and Lindsey to remove their shirts, Stevie initially refused. Lindsey grew angry and told her to stop being "a child"—that what they were doing was "for art." Stevie relented. The resulting black-and-white image showed a portion of Stevie's right breast hidden behind Lindsey's bare shoulder.

And to add insult to injury, Polydor misspelled Stevie's name as "Stevi" in the album credits and on the album jacket.

"I was crying when we took that picture," Stevie said. "And Lindsey was mad at me. He said, 'You know, you're just being a child. This is art.' And I'm going, 'This is not art. This is me taking a nude photograph with you, and I don't dig it.' I thought, 'Who are you? Don't you know me?' . . . I couldn't breathe. But I did it because I felt like a rat in a trap."

Stevie channeled her frustration into a song called "Garbo," a *Wild Heart* outtake that would later show up on her 1998 *The Enchanted Works of Stevie Nicks* box set. The spare, waltzing ballad intentionally compared Stevie to Greta Garbo, a 1930s starlet who famously refused to wear anything revealing on screen. "Every time I tell this story I feel like I'm depressing the audience," Stevie later said onstage when she performed "Garbo" on her 1998 Enchanted tour. "At the same time, I need to absolutely tell you what happened. I went to do this, I was not happy about it. I got in a lot of trouble for not being happy about it. 'Don't be paranoid, don't be a child. This is art.' I was very young. In my dramatic way, I thought, 'Maybe the movie stars who came here felt this way. Maybe they felt like they had to do something they didn't want to do that much, but they did it anyway for art, for music.'"

Stevie swore to herself that she'd never be put in that kind of position ever again—not by Lindsey, not by anybody. "From the very beginning, Lindsey was very controlling and very possessive," she said later. "And after hearing all the stories from my mother and how independent she'd made me, I was never very good with controlling people and possessive people."

Even more frustrating, Lindsey and Stevie's debut album did not perform anywhere near as well as they'd hoped. With little to no promotion behind it, *Buckingham Nicks* landed with a thud. Radio DJs told Polydor's promotion team that they disliked Stevie's voice, which they described as too nasal. None of the major music magazines like *Rolling Stone* and *Creem* cared to review it. There was a silver lining, however—when Buckingham Nicks toured the American south, they found their record had a cult following in Birmingham, Alabama, because the local rock station had been spinning tracks from *Buckingham Nicks*. Still, Polydor unceremoniously dropped the duo the following year.

They were back at square one—and out of money (again). Stevie's romantic relationship with Lindsey was on the rocks. Another layer to her pain was that grandpa A.J. had recently died. As Stevie went back to waitressing, she seriously contemplated whether she wanted to keep pursuing music. "Lindsey went back to writing his angst-laden songs, and I went back to being a waitress," Stevie said. "I didn't mind being a waitress—but we couldn't believe it! We thought we had made it!" Stevie's father thought she should come back home and try something else. But Barbara Nicks would remind Stevie: "Remember, you're on a *mission*."

Stevie was also incredibly lonely. While Lindsey connected with other LA-based musicians like Warren Zevon, Waddy, and Jorge Calderon, Stevie's work schedule kept her from making many close friends, unlike the thriving community she'd built in the Bay Area.

Joni Mitchell's *Court and Spark* album kept Stevie company during this time. In 2011, Stevie told *The Guardian* how she spent much of that year gloomily listening to Mitchell's sixth studio album and contemplating her life. "Lindsey and I were coming to the end of our relationship, and I'd met someone else," she remembered. "I latched on to the title track, which is about a new relationship that doesn't last. . . . It was the only time I ever felt music might not work out. I talked to my parents about going back to school, because I was tired of being a cleaning lady, a waitress, and a rock 'n' roll star at the same time. We were really poor. At the same time, we were already living in the world that Joni Mitchell was writing about because our producer, Keith Olsen, had introduced us to a lot of people in the industry. I related to a song like 'The Same Situation' whenever I'd go to a party and music business sharks were everywhere. They would look at me as the blonde who could sing and might make lots of money for someone. I didn't like being looked at as a commodity."

Stevie's halting—and at times humiliating—rise to rock stardom is a classic LA success story. Every year, thousands of young dreamers and creatives move to the city with stars in their eyes, hoping against hope that they'll beat the odds and make a name for themselves in their chosen industry. You don't even have to have creative aspirations or want to live in a big city to understand what Stevie went through at this stage. Anyone who has started at the bottom rung can relate; every industry has its politics, power trips, and inherent imbalances. Run into enough of them early on and you'll no doubt spend the next few years wondering what the hell you're even doing.

One of Stevie's most enduring songs, "Landslide," captured those purgatorial months after Buckingham Nicks was dropped from the Polydor label. Stevie had "built [her] life around" Lindsey, first in Fritz and later as a singing duo. After their debut album went nowhere, Lindsey was fielding offers to play on the road while Stevie continued odd-jobbing. What did her future look like if it wasn't with him? She would find out much later, as they broke up and Stevie embarked on a solo career, but "Landslide" reveals how early she was asking herself important questions about where life would ultimately take her.

Stevie's parents were even more worried about their daughter, who sounded sickly and exhausted every time they spoke on the phone. Stevie's father tried reasoning with his daughter again during a visit to Los Angeles, suggesting that she give it six more months, and if it didn't work out, then maybe she should consider going back and finishing college. Something about that timetable renewed Stevie's resolve. Marching into the apartment she shared with Lindsey, Stevie demanded that they push even harder to resurrect Buckingham Nicks. "I wrote 'Landslide' about whether or not I was going to give it all one more chance," she said. "You know the rest of the story."

In the fall of 1974, after hundreds of houses cleaned, dining tables wiped, and one broken recording contract, Stevie's patience and persistence finally paid off.

Back at Sound City, Keith Olsen played the Buckingham Nicks song "Frozen Love" for Mick Fleetwood, the founding drummer (and partial namesake) of Fleetwood Mac, a British blues-rock-turned-pop outfit that had been putting out albums and touring since 1967. Mick immediately liked what he heard. Would Mick like to meet Lindsey, Keith asked? The two future bandmates shook hands. A couple of weeks later, Mick called Keith wondering whether Lindsey would ever consider joining Fleetwood Mac. Maybe, Keith said. But if you want Lindsey, you also have to hire Stevie. They're a package deal.

The timing (for once) was impeccable. Just as Stevie was out there wondering whether she should remain in Los Angeles, Fleetwood Mac had recently relocated to Los Angeles at the urging of their guitarist Bob Welch, who was strongly considering leaving the band after two years. Long before Stevie and Lindsey joined, Fleetwood Mac had famously revolved through several other members after launching with founding members Mick Fleetwood, John McVie, and Peter Green, who, along with guitarist Jeremy Spencer, infused the project with a psychedelic twist across early albums like *Mr. Wonderful* and *The Pious Bird of Good Omen*.

But by the early 1970s, however, Fleetwood Mac was also in purgatory. Various members had come and left due to creative differences, intraband affairs, or drug use. Founding guitarist Peter had left the band after wrapping their European tour in spring 1970; bassist John McVie brought in his wife, former Chicken Shack member Christine Perfect, on vocals and keyboards a few months later. Following a U.S. tour in February 1971, Jeremy Spencer abruptly left the band to join the Children of God, a religious group. Founding guitarist Danny Kirwan had developed a severe alcohol dependency and was fired.

Fleetwood Mac carried on for a while, hiring Bob Weston on guitar and Dave Walker on vocals, but the group hit a roadblock again when drummer Mick Fleetwood realized Bob had been having an affair with Mick's then wife, Jenny Boyd. The band had also taken legal action against their former manager, Clifford Davis, to prevent him from using the group's name for another set of musicians. By the time Stevie and Lindsey came into the picture, the future of Fleetwood Mac was a giant question mark.

At first, Lindsey wasn't so sure about joining; the guitarist

It's hard to keep the sparkly going when you face so many closed doors. But somewhere in my heart I knew that it would work out and that if I kept making enough money to pay the rent, Lindsey would hang in there and get better and better on guitar and keep learning about the business.

worried that a collective environment might overwhelm and diminish his frontman persona. But Stevie urged patience. "We can always quit," she told her partner. "They're going to pay us two hundred dollars each a week, so we can save some money and leave in six months with a little nest egg if it doesn't work."

From the outside, it might have looked as if Mick Fleetwood came galloping up on a white horse to rescue the floundering duo, and that might have been true from a financial perspective. But Stevie had more obstacles to clear than her creative counterpart. For starters, she needed to convince pretty much everybody that she wasn't *just* an accessory to Lindsey Buckingham, who had been the primary draw. What's more, a middling *Rolling Stone* review of Fleetwood Mac's 1975 album (her first with the group) had stuck with her, so much so that she'd wanted to quit outright. Later, while promoting *Rumours,* she could recite the most negative passages of that review to Cameron Crowe when he profiled her.

"They said my singing was 'callow' and that really hurt my feelings," Stevie said. "Time after time I would read: '. . . the raucous voice of Stevie Nicks and the golden-throated voice of Christine McVie, who's the only saving grace of the band.' When it comes to competition, I won't compete for a man, and I won't compete for a place on that stage either. If I'm not wanted, I'll get out. I was bummed."

Turns out, one so-so *Rolling Stone* review didn't decide the new Fleetwood Mac (or Stevie's) fate. Their reintroduction album went gold, and when "Rhiannon" was released as a single the following year, it got enormous airplay and peaked at number 11 on the U.S. charts.

Stevie couldn't have known that her and Lindsey's addition to Fleetwood Mac would send the entire band on a rocketship into the celebrity stratosphere; they'd go on to become one of the bestselling acts of all time and be inducted into the Rock and Roll Hall of Fame. Their second album all together, *Rumours,* would win Album of the Year at the 1978 Grammy Awards.

It takes a lot of daring to chase your dreams. Fear is unavoidable if you're trying to achieve anything, if you're stretching beyond your comfort zone. Not to mention those raised eyebrows you encounter when you share your audacious goals. Those reactions feed the fear and make you wonder if it's really wise to spend your precious time and energy on a big, uncertain pursuit. Because the truth is, you *could* pour your all into a goal and still fail. When is it right to take a risk?

How could Stevie have known that her drive, goals, and ambition were justified? When I look at the choices she made in the face of industry rejection and Hollywood sycophantism—a landscape she chronicled in the soaring soft rock ballad "After the Glitter Fades," which she wrote in 1972 and later placed on *Bella Donna*—I see a woman with tremendous trust in herself. It seems to me that Stevie knew she had a gift and she knew she could trust herself. She didn't know how things would play out, and she didn't always know that she'd make it in Hollywood, but what kept her going was her self-knowledge and self-assurance.

When any of us faces challenges and naysayers, we'd do well to channel her words of determination: "What I seem to want, well, you know I'll find a way."

LESSON THREE

TELL THE TRUTH, ALWAYS

From the very beginning, I said, I think I even said this to my mom, I'm never going to be dishonest in my songs. If he broke up with me, I'm not going to write the song and say I broke up with him. I'm never going to not tell the truth.

—Stevie Nicks, 2011

Stevie Nicks is nothing if not a truth teller. Across a half century's worth of songs and interviews, speeches and stories, she is famously unflinching in her honesty.

Now, let's not get it twisted—"truth telling" doesn't mean proselytizing or calling up that one family member or frustrating co-worker to tell them exactly what you think of them. Truth telling does not necessarily mean forgoing all tact.

The most vital type of truth telling, as Stevie has exemplified, is simply telling the truth about yourself, to yourself and any concerned parties. Have the gumption and bravery to get to know yourself on a cellular level. The number of people who lie to themselves about who they are and what they really want is staggering. But if we learn anything from Stevie's life, it's that she really knows herself in ways that are profound.

Stevie's candidness presented vividly in interviews, particularly in the early eighties, when she embarked on a solo career. Ironically, she didn't give many long interviews in those first few Fleetwood Mac years, and when she did, she often sounded, well, high or drunk out of her mind. (As has been endlessly documented, every member of Fleetwood Mac notoriously indulged in various forms of rock 'n' roll excess. "In the studio, we had a ritual, in which the engineers and band members all started humming a tune—it changed over the years—which would serve as a siren's call for cocaine, specifically the cocaine that I was invariably holding," Mick Fleetwood wrote in his 2014 memoir.)

Once Stevie took center stage in the media, you never got the sense that she was giving the journalist canned or manufactured answers. There might be subjects she preferred to stay away from, such as her love and sex life, but she could wax philosophical for hours on a variety of subjects.

"I said a long time ago, I would not hedge," Stevie told the still new MTV in 1983 around the release of her sophomore solo album, *Wild Heart*. "If I was going to be a writer, I was going to write down the truth. I wasn't going to name names, and I wasn't going to be unkind, but I was going to tell the truth. I don't have any reason not to [tell the truth], and if I am going to write and . . . make these songs [about] experiences that I know every one of you has had, then when you have that experience and you hear that song, you'll click into it and you will know exactly what I am talking about."

A few years after that, while promoting her fourth solo album, *The Other Side of the Mirror,* Stevie reiterated her disinterest in "nam[ing] names" but promised the interviewer that she would always be truthful in her material. "I do dress [my songs up], and I do make them more flamboyant, and I do bring the sparkle into them. But underneath them all, if you listen very carefully, is the real story. I'm not going to say 'and

If I was going to be a writer, I was going to write down the truth.

this was him, and this was her. . . .' I'm never going to do that because that's not my purpose of writing. I go ahead with the story, but I don't name names."

Truth—or a version of it, depending on the songwriter—was the primary ingredient in nearly every successful Fleetwood Mac record. Anyone who followed the pop collective in the 1970s and ensuing decades knows that the group, then comprising Nicks, guitarist (and Nicks's onetime paramour) Lindsey Buckingham, drummer Mick Fleetwood, keyboardist Christine McVie, and bassist John McVie, never held back from chronicling their tumultuous romances with one another on their albums. In fact, when I was a kid, my dad introduced me to Fleetwood Mac by talking about how its members were so disastrously entangled with one another that it ultimately contributed to their undoing. "It's what happens when you have too many talented people in one band," he said as we listened to Fleetwood Mac's greatest hits in the family Volvo station wagon.

Stevie's innermost thoughts and conflicts found their way into her songwriting from the start of her recording career. On "Long Distance Winner," which appeared on *Buckingham Nicks,* Stevie processed her complicated feelings about being with Lindsey. "What the song is really all about is a difficult artist saying 'I adore you, but you're difficult, and I'll stay here with you, but you're still difficult,'" she said in 1998.

As even the most casual Fleetwood Mac fan would come to know, Lindsey and Stevie developed a reputation for writing bracing, brutal songs about each other, and they'd perform those songs side by side to audiences of thousands. If you think this arrangement was peaceful, well, you'd be wrong. But in the midseventies, especially as they were invited to join Fleetwood Mac, Stevie and Lindsey's joint ambition overrode any embarrassment they might have felt. After all, a potential hit song was a potential hit song.

When Stevie and Lindsey were invited to be in Fleetwood Mac, they were so thrilled that they agreed to give the romantic side of their relationship another shot. "Maybe we're not going to have any more problems, because we're finally going to have some money," Stevie reasoned.

But with this new opportunity came new problems in their relationship. The rest of the band noticed that Lindsey had a controlling dynamic with Stevie, who seemed to defer to him in most things. As Stevie's famously fervent live performances of "Rhiannon" took form, Lindsey acted put out, telling her she was being too sexy. Plus, Stevie had some brewing sexual tension with Mick Fleetwood, who'd thought she was beautiful from the moment he first saw her at Sound City. By the end of 1975, Lindsey and Stevie had broken up for good. But they still had to play in Fleetwood Mac together.

In the wake of her split from Lindsey, Stevie wrote the era-defining single "Dreams." "I handed a cassette of the song to Lindsey," Nicks said in 2009. "It was a rough take, just me singing solo and playing piano. Even though he was mad with me at the time, Lindsey played it and then looked up at me and smiled. What was going on between us was sad—we were [a couple] who couldn't make it through. But as musicians, we still respected each other." (Lindsey, naturally, put in his two cents about the couple's breakup on the also sizable Mac hit "Go Your Own Way," in which he appeared to acknowledge his inability to commit.)

"Dreams" would hardly be the only Stevie-led track on which the singer mined her broken relationship with Lindsey for material. Their doomed romance would be a continuous theme across several of her songs, both in Fleetwood Mac and solo. On the urgent "Planets of the Universe," which started as a *Rumours* demo but eventually made its way onto the singer's 2001 solo album *Trouble in Shangri-La,* Nicks processed the relationship through some of her favorite mediums: spirituality and elemental imagery.

However, few Stevie-led songs were as profoundly truthful as "Landslide." A lasting showcase of Stevie's inherent songwriting talent and wisdom, "Landslide" dealt with matters internal and external, looking within to consider Stevie's collapsing relationship with Lindsey and zooming out to examine more existential concerns about life, career, and purpose.

"Landslide" grew out of a moment when Stevie was back to waiting tables while Lindsey got invited to go on tour with the Everly Brothers. Before the tour kicked off, the couple drove to Aspen, Colorado, where Lindsey would rehearse for two weeks with Don Everly. After Lindsey left, Stevie decided to stick around Aspen for a few months. Surrounded by the Rocky Mountains, which would provide the imagery for the "snow-covered hills" of "Landslide," Stevie felt more listless and depressed than ever. "I was in Aspen with forty dollars and my dog and my Toyota that went frozen the day we got there," Stevie said. "We thought [Lindsey] was going to make lots of money. He didn't."

Fortunately, the house Stevie was staying in had a piano. With her guitar in tow, Stevie sat in the living room, looked out at the mountains, and wrote "Landslide," which in its spare, acoustic-led melody emphasized Stevie's robust alto and anxious inner monologue as she faced down her future and wondered out loud whether her big dreams of rock success and stardom would ever materialize.

In our most difficult moments, we can all relate to the anxiety spiral, which tends to start small—an overdrafted account, an unanswered email, an undercommunicative partner—before tumbling into the abyss. (Some questions in the existential black hole: What's this all for? Where am I going? How much control do I have over anything? Not that this writer would know anything about that . . .)

Stevie's circumstances might have been unique, but the song they inspired held a universal truth—that everyone, regardless of where they come from or how old they are, wonders from time to time whether they're on the right path. Everyone, to some degree or another, struggles with the idea of change.

Stevie had the innate ability to look inward, self-reflect, and be honest at a profoundly uncertain time of her life. There were no guarantees that "Landslide" or any of the other dozens of songs she'd written in the early 1970s would ever see the light of day. There were no promises that she'd ever get picked up by another record label or even generate enough gig work to justify another night of songwriting. No doubt the many artists who covered "Landslide" in the decades that followed (Tori Amos, the Smashing Pumpkins, the Chicks) could relate.

Even if Stevie had never continued down her path to Fleetwood Mac or solo stardom, she would still be a consummate truth teller. Like so many singer-songwriters whose work resonates with audiences on a global scale, the act of writing down her lived experiences helped Stevie gain clarity on everything from career stall-outs to crumbling relationships.

A decade later, sitting on the couch for an interview on MTV, Stevie went on to explain why she felt compelled to write about the blood and guts within her life and the famously fraught intraband dynamics in Fleetwood Mac, which came out in full force on 1977's *Rumours*. "No one knows unless you really look. That's the people I write for, because someone needs to write about what is happening to all of us."

Rumours, which remains the defining Fleetwood Mac album, offered a soap-operatic snapshot of a band threading the needle between perfect pop chemistry and utter emotional disarray. (Plus, add in scads of drugs.) As Stevie and Lindsey were breaking up (and writing messy songs about said breakup), Christine and John McVie, who had been married for eight years, were also on the outs, with Christine openly dating the band's lighting director. Behind the drum kit, Mick Fleetwood was going through his own marriage drama with Jenny Boyd. Each primary songwriter—Christine, Stevie, and Lindsey—wrote the drama right into *Rumours*.

"On this album, all the songs that I wrote except maybe 'Gold Dust Woman'—and even that comes into it—are definitely about the people in the band. . . . Chris's relationships, John's relationship, Mick's relationship, Lindsey's and mine," Stevie told *Rolling Stone*. "They're all there and they're very honest and people will know exactly what I'm talking about . . . people will really enjoy listening to what happened since the last album."

To Stevie, it's the truth that makes for the most powerful and discerning songwriting. *Rumours* as an album had such a tidal-wave effect on the music industry and all of pop culture that scores of newer songwriters have followed in its stead. In 2023, Stevie told TODAY.com that she thought her friend and famously diaristic lyricist Taylor Swift had taken to heart her advice to write truthfully. "I never don't tell the truth. And I think that's something that if Taylor Swift, who is my friend, if Taylor got anything from me, that's what she got. I don't ever lie in my songs—if you broke up with me, I don't put I broke up with you. I tell the truth, always.

"I think that's maybe why my songs connect with people," Stevie continued. "Because I'm telling them their own story. Everything that happens to me, basically happens to everybody else, in just different ways, different forms, but nevertheless, it's the same premise. . . . You fall in love. Somebody breaks up with you. Your heart is broken. You break up with them, their heart is broken. You feel bad because you broke up with them and their heart is broken and vice versa. And that's really the Shakespearean tragedy of most love songs. And then of course your mom says, 'You'll get through it, you always do.' And you do."

LESSON FOUR

BELIEVE IN CRYSTAL VISIONS

I don't think that I consciously have premonitions, but I do seem to have some sort of a psychic knowledge of what's gonna happen in the future.

—Stevie Nicks, VH1 Storytellers, 1998

Dreams, visions, and intuition have long played a vital role in Stevie's lyricism, whether she was singing of love and relationships, witches and goddesses, or a global need for human kindness.

In a stroke of literalism, Stevie has theorized that her "visions" are partially a result of her having terribly poor eyesight. "I definitely perceive the world differently than most people do," Stevie acknowledged in 1983. "I have really bad eyes, and I never wore glasses, you see. . . . Then all of a sudden, I got contact lenses—soft ones, which don't make you see great but make you see better. Now I'm completely confused. I used to see nothing. Now I see, sort of. Everything is either a blur or it's psychedelic or more acid-like. Streetlights sparkle, colors run together. But because I can't see the world clearly, I look at it differently. I see it like in a dream."

Instead of correcting her blurry vision, Stevie brought audiences into her kaleidoscopic universe through any number of songs, both with Fleetwood Mac and solo. Like an astrologer or a psychic medium, Stevie seemed to exist in a celestial dimension beyond this plane, even if her lyrics were catalyzed by a real person or event. (She would probably attribute this duality to her being a Gemini.) Regardless of their exact origin, Stevie's visions and premonitions have blurred into the imaginary, the mythical, the otherworldly, the folkloric—and provided her audiences hundreds of teachable moments.

Today, Stevie has a playful reputation in popular culture as being downright clairvoyant. But let's cut back to Stevie at twenty-six years old, just before she joined Fleetwood Mac. In a previous chapter, we talked about how much Stevie loved listening to Joni Mitchell's *Court and Spark* while toiling away at menial jobs in Los Angeles. But what I didn't mention was that Stevie was high on LSD ("the only time I ever did it," she claimed in Stephen Davis's biography *Gold Dust Woman*) as she immersed herself into Joni's seminal album.

Feeling low and searching for a note of clarity, Stevie put *Court and Spark* on at Keith Olsen's house and spent the next three straight days listening to Joni describe the double standards and drawbacks to being a female rock star in an unforgiving city like Los Angeles. "You have two options," Joni told *Rolling Stone* at that time. "You can stay the same and protect the formula that gave you your initial success. They're going to crucify you for staying the same. If you change, they're going to crucify you for changing. But staying the same is boring. And change is interesting. So, of the two options, I'd rather be crucified for changing."

Over those three days, Stevie got the insight she so badly needed in the form of a premonition—that's when she wrote what would become her signature song, one that tells the story of an otherworldly Night Queen with the power of the divine feminine. A goddess destined to capture attention—

but at what cost? Stevie decided to call this beguiling figure Rhiannon, a name she felt drawn to after reading it in Mary Bartlet Leader's 1973 book *Triad: A Novel of the Supernatural*.

Stevie paired the name Rhiannon with a more down-to-earth refrain that had been circling through her mind: "Will you ever win?" Stevie sent that simple question out into the universe, wondering whether she and Lindsey would ever conquer the city that had supplied them with possibility but seemed to be denying them success at every turn.

Stevie had a way of bending dreams, visions, and premonitions in all different directions, making it so that no one song was ever about exactly one thing (or person). For instance, Fleetwood Mac's "Dreams" *was* at its core a breakup song about Lindsey Buckingham, but it also examined the word "dreams" through the lens of ambition. Stevie acknowledged subverting her own "crystal visions" for Lindsey's benefit. On one hand, she knew better than anyone else how badly Lindsey craved rock star success, yet she cautioned him against staying too long at the fair. Fame's higher plane was not sustainable. All those women who wanted to be with him now that he was famous? Their affection was conditional. In a quieter moment, he'd surely remember what he had—and what he'd lost. As downhearted as "Dreams" was, it also managed to be tentatively optimistic. "I always put something at the end that says there's hope," Stevie said. "You know, 'When the rain washes you clean you'll know.' And that's an old [Native American] custom . . . that if it rains, their spirit is set free."

Because I can't see the world clearly, I look at it differently. I see it like in a dream.

As time went on, Stevie grew even more confident in letting her visions tell stories. In 1981, she designed the bewitching cover of her debut solo album *Bella Donna* from, as *Rolling Stone* eloquently put it in 1981, "a somnambulant brainstorm."

"I dreamed that I saw, against a background of blue, a white vertical line, which was me holding a bird," Stevie told the writer Timothy White, who traveled to LA to profile the singer after recording concluded. "At five in the morning I called up Paul Fishkin [her former boyfriend and founder, with Danny Goldberg, of her label, Modern Records]. I described to him the image, which became the front cover, and then the one on the back, where I've picked up the tambourine and the roses, and I'm looking through the crystal tambourine, which symbolizes a porthole, to see the sorrows of the world. I love the symbolism of the three roses, which is very pyramid, very Maya. The white outfit I'm wearing is the exact opposite of my black outfit on *Rumours*. Over that it says, 'Come in from the darkness.'"

Fantasy played a vital role, too, on Stevie's fourth solo album, 1989's *The Other Side of the Mirror,* which plainly references Lewis Carroll's beloved book *Through the Looking-Glass, and What Alice Found*

There. At first, the project was inspired by Stevie's grandmother, whom the family called Crazy Alice.

"I love making up little fantasy things," Stevie said. "All the characters in my songs . . . they're all me. But they're all different sides of me. It's a great way to write about what's going on in your life without telling it in a real serious way, but the point comes over and I think people understand that. I don't think I started out intending it to have much to do with *Alice in Wonderland,* though I read it when I was little. But I kept thinking about how I go back and forth from one side of the mirror to the other. And then I have a little space in between, which is when I do other things which nobody really knows about; my painting, my art, my writing."

Even as recently as 2020, Stevie spoke at length about how her solo single "Show Them the Way" was inspired by an especially vivid dream she'd had ahead of the 2008 presidential election. While staying in St. Charles, Illinois, Stevie dreamed she'd been invited to perform at a political benefit attended by John F. Kennedy and Martin Luther King, Jr. She later recalled to the *Los Angeles Times* that in this dream, MLK was leading her by the arm into a ballroom where the Kennedy brothers and John Lewis were seated. When she woke, Stevie was so moved that she immediately wrote the experience into song.

Then, toward the end of "Show Them the Way," Stevie envisioned a shadow. The figure reminded her: "Don't forget what we were fighting for," a quote Stevie's mother had repeated throughout her life.

Later, Stevie told ABC Audio that she probably dreamed of these twentieth-century leaders because, at the time, she'd been watching a lot of political documentaries. "[It felt] so real . . . I feel it's probably the only dream I ever had that actually had a beginning, a middle, and an end, and I totally remembered every little bit of it."

"Show Them the Way" nearly appeared on Stevie's 2011 album, literally titled *In Your Dreams,* but ultimately she didn't feel that it went with the rest of the record. "I said, 'Okay, I totally get it, and it really doesn't go with the rest of these songs, it would be an outlier on this,'" she said, adding that 2020, a tumultuous year caught between a catastrophic global pandemic and racial protesting, felt like a more appropriate time to release it. "I think the world is calling for it right now."

As children, we're encouraged to dream big, chase interests and ambitions, and indulge in fantasy worlds. As we age, however, that encouragement from elders flips around into suggestions that we grow up and be sensible. If we like to spend time interpreting our dreams, hey, you're being woo-woo. If we love to read (or write) fantasy, we might be accused of arrested development. Activities like art, music, and writing are dismissed as hobbies intended for leisure time, if you can scrape any together after the workday ends and the kids go to bed. But there are tremendous gifts to be gained by living as Stevie does, with one foot in unreality. Who knows where it might lead, what you'll create, or how you might feel. "Thank you for believing in crystal visions," Stevie later told a breathless audience as Fleetwood Mac accepted their star on the Hollywood Walk of Fame in 1979. "Crystal visions really do come true."

LESSON FIVE

LIVE IN A WORLD OF MAGIC

I love haunting, haunted melodies. I've never been, and probably never will be, a down-home rock 'n' roll songwriter. I try to add that extra, spooky dimension to whatever I do. I want my songs to sort of step a little bit into the bizarre.

—Stevie Nicks, Us magazine, 1980

Fifty-odd years after Stevie Nicks came to pop culture prominence, it's a little funny now to think about how many people panicked about her "witchy woman" persona, which was enhanced by her body-shaking performances of "Rhiannon." And if they didn't panic, they eye-rolled her as being too California-girl woo-woo—not anything to take very seriously.

I was especially struck by a 1980 interview in the *New Musical Express* in which the journalist Chris Salewicz openly mocked Stevie's fan-ascribed designation as "the *mystical* member of Fleetwood Mac" and said her "(un)enlightenment" sounds like "a product of the Guru of the Month Club."

Other interviews were much more open-minded. When Daisann McLane profiled Fleetwood Mac that same year, she appeared to be swept up in the mysticism: "The more I learn about the members of Fleetwood Mac and their entourage, the more I find myself struggling with notions I thought I dismissed years ago: karma, destiny, karass, hand of fate."

Audiences started picking up on Stevie's magic when Fleetwood Mac released "Rhiannon," which Stevie always introduced live as being "a song about an old Welsh witch." Her accompanying onstage sway, heavy, curtained bangs, and sheer black chiffon dress made Stevie's midseventies performances of "Rhiannon" instantly iconic, a crowd favorite.

"'Rhiannon' is the heavy-duty song to sing every night," Stevie told *Crawdaddy* in 1976. "Onstage it's really a mind-tripper. Everybody, including me, is just blitzed by the end of it. And I put out so much in that song that I'm nearly down. There's something to that song that touches people. I don't know what it is, but I'm really glad it happened."

When Stevie would perform "Rhiannon" engulfed in flowing black capes and twirling with her tambourine, sometimes a full moon in the sky behind her, rock critics responded with a mix of wonder, bewilderment, and (again) dismissal. Who—or what—was this unknowable cipher? (Worse, as Lester Bangs wrote in a 1977 issue of *Creem,* Stevie was "an airhead, a puffball.")

When journalists had the chance to spend time with Stevie in more mundane moments, they noted how she decorated her surroundings in old-fashioned chintzy style. Daisann McLane's 1980 *Rolling Stone* cover story, for example, observed her post-root-canal, "propped up in a mountain of pillows" in an "antique four-poster with a thick mattress about three feet high." McLane compares her to *The Princess and the Pea,* or a lady of Victorian England who "believes in faeries," "keeps a journal," and writes "sentimental fiction and poetry." None of these attributes seems remotely out of pocket for a performer today, but in the late seventies and early eighties, culture at large was still struggling to comprehend the previous two decades, which had challenged convention in every possible sense.

Of course five-foot-one Stevie, always cold and draped in diaphanous fabrics, always writing higher-vibrational songs about mythological creatures, probably appeared like a practitioner of the occult. (To be clear, she wasn't—and isn't.) But people tend to villainize what they don't understand. As Stevie's star rose with Fleetwood Mac's, some authority figures chaffed at her witchy appearance, believing her to be a Satan worshipper.

This misinformation went on for decades. In 1998, a music minister named Scott Naden of Southwood Presbyterian church in Huntsville, Alabama, banned five seniors from playing "Landslide" at Huntsville High School's baccalaureate program. "I can't believe people are still telling me I'm a witch because I wear black," she scoffed in a public statement, adding via her manager that she was "tired" of denying her being a witch, and that people should "just get a life."

"In the beginning of my career, the whole idea that some wacky, creepy people were writing, 'You're a witch, you're a witch!' was so arresting," Stevie also told the *Los Angeles Times* in 2014. "And there I am like, 'No, I'm not! I just wear black because it makes me look thinner, you idiots.'"

Instead of shying away from accusations of witchcraft (save for an interview here and there in which she'd outright dismiss the concept), Stevie leaned in harder with songs like "Sorcerer," which she wrote in 1972 with Buckingham Nicks and gave to Marilyn Martin for the 1984 *Streets of Fire* soundtrack before releasing her own version in 2001 on *Trouble in Shangri-La.*

While "Sorcerer" on its face echoed Stevie's long-standing use of mystical imagery, the solo deep cut had its feet firmly planted in reality, as it looked back at the moment Stevie and Lindsey first arrived in Los Angeles. "['Sorcerer'] was really about the city of Hollywood and how strange it was to us," Stevie revealed in 2001. "It was all about models and rock 'n' roll and drugs and scary people. I was a very, very prudish little girl from San Francisco who had strict parents, I had not had a lot of freedom, and coming into this town was freaky. 'All around the black ink darkness, and who found the lady from the mountains?' The lady from the mountains was me."

That's the key, and it's a simple, classic one: Stevie loves to use magic as metaphor. "Stevie's mysticism was entirely self-taught," the publicist Danny Goldberg later wrote of his friend. "Not for her studies of Blake, Rimbaud, Ginsberg, nor even the Bible. She was an autodidactic mystic who viewed the universe through the eyes of a middle American."

Stevie might literally believe in fairies, angels, good witches, and spirits, but her belief in the supernatural and alternate planes of reality doesn't prevent her from understanding the one we all share here on earth. If anything, her descriptions of magic and onstage transcendence became a lexicon for communicating a universal experience. For instance, on the Stevie-penned, Fleetwood Mac–released *Tango in the Night* single "Seven Wonders," Stevie invoked spiritual language to describe a powerful love affair.

Stevie also took a particular interest in the idea of past lives. As Stephen Davis recounted in *Gold Dust Woman,* the singer had a "life reading" with a mystic in the mideighties in which she was informed that her previous incarnations included a high priestess in ancient Egypt, a famous concert pianist, and a German "who went through some of the atrocities." Stevie also found out that the life she was currently on would be her final one. (Psychic mediums tend to agree that people who opt out of parenthood are likely on their last reincarnation, as are people who express a deep interest in spirituality and personal growth.)

It's not as if magic as a metaphor is so unusual; after all, how many songs can you list off the top of your head with "Magic" in the title? "Magic" by the Cars; "Magic Carpet Ride" by Steppenwolf; "Magic Man" by Heart; "Do You Believe in Magic?" by the Lovin' Spoonful; "This Magic Moment" by the Drifters. It's practically a cliché, and it certainly wasn't anything new by the time Fleetwood Mac gained a mass following in 1975. But Stevie's songwriting and performance style introduced a new way of expressing the metaphysical and weaving it into audiences' lived experiences.

"There is always magic to be summoned at any point," Stevie told Los Angeles radio DJ Jim Ladd in 1979. "I love to live in a world of magic, but not a fake world of magic. We all really basically have a lot of magic. . . . It's only those of us that choose to accept it, that really understand it. It's there for everyone. That's the only thing that I feel that I am able to give to people and that's why I know that they respond to me, because I try to give them only their own magic . . . not mine, but theirs."

By 1983, Stevie must have grown used to interviewers asking her in any number of ways about her belief in magic, visions, fairies, and anything related. When an MTV interviewer asked her point-blank—"You once said you were a witch"—Stevie, possibly a little drug-addled, made light of the question without really answering it. "I lied. Or just in the funny sense . . . like the silly witch that crashes into your window on the broom."

Stevie winkingly leaned into her witch persona by appearing in Ryan Murphy's horror drama *American Horror Story: Coven*. In a 2014 episode called "The Magical Delights of Stevie Nicks," Stevie made her acting debut as "the White Witch" and sang "Rhiannon" at the piano. Ironically, she almost didn't take the cameo, telling *Vulture* how in 1977 she'd started getting "some really stupid wacky mail from witchy weirdos" who seemed to think she really belonged to a coven.

There is always
magic to be
summoned
at any point.

"I didn't like it. I'd only been famous for two years, and it scared me. So I had some colored outfits made. I wore red and green and salmon for a year, and then I said, 'Well, this is not going to work for me, so I'm going back to black,' and I did."

In her trademark pragmatic way, Stevie also realized the upside of appearing on a show like *American Horror Story:* "This is taking my music to a generation of kids from fifteen to forty that have never really probably been associated with it."

While she clearly had some hesitation going into filming, Stevie took the opportunity to face any lingering anxieties. "When all this came along, I was like, 'What, really, am I going to turn this down because of all that past nonsense?'" she told the *Los Angeles Times*. "I'm way too old and I've been through way too much to give up an opportunity like this. I'm fearless. You have to be fearless in life. I'm not afraid of anything. Don't you ever be afraid of anything."

Wear black if you want. Let them call you a witch, and believe whatever you want to believe. And don't be afraid to laugh at yourself sometimes, too.

LESSON SIX

FLOAT IN LIKE GODDESSES

I believe that there is a certain amount of mysticism that all women should have, that you should never tell all your secrets, that you should never tell everybody all about you. I never have.

—Stevie Nicks, SPIN magazine, 1997

The moment Stevie Nicks started to perform with Fleetwood Mac in a rotating array of flowy black shawls and bell-sleeved gowns, capes and velvet platform boots, top hats, and tambourines fluttering with ribbons, she inspired a fashion movement that would define an era and extend through the next half century. If you don't believe me, google "stevie nicks fashion" and let the infinite pages of boho-inspired accessories and suggestions wash over you.

As Fleetwood Mac's global popularity rose out of the free-love sixties, an unconstrained decade uniquely defined by the rejection of the previous generation's rules, Stevie's moodier take on hippie bohemian style felt perfectly timed to the moment, which also leaned into women's liberation through unconstrained styles and fabrics. As the decades passed, Stevie's style would evolve from homespun hippie fairy to something much darker and more gothic, featuring black capes dripping with crystal beads and other jewels. Regardless of how her look shifted, however, it was always uniquely her own.

Later in life, when asked about her style evolution—particularly her tendency to wear all black—Stevie would maintain that it wasn't that deep. By always wearing black, she simply didn't have to think as hard about matching colors. (That, and black was slimming.)

Stevie had been thinking about her personal style ever since her Bay Area days in Fritz. In 1981, she told *Glamour* about the show they opened for Janis Joplin, who also tended to perform in the era-appropriate uniform of boho blouses and dresses. Looking out into the audience from backstage, eighteen-year-old Stevie noticed a young woman in the audience "wearing a mauvy pink chiffon skirt and very high cream suede boots. Her hair was kind of Gibson [Girl]. She had some pink ribbons—and I thought that's *it*."

Stevie felt similarly inspired by a tiny vintage store in downtown San Francisco called the Velvet Underground. This was where "all the rock 'n' roll girls got their clothes once they could afford it," she later told audiences in Manchester in 2015. Even if Stevie didn't have the funds to shop at the hip city boutiques, just knowing that her heroes like Janis Joplin had set foot in there was inspiration enough. Imagining her favorites floating through the Velvet Underground to select stage attire fueled her mission. Some way, somehow, Stevie's own dreams of rock stardom would come true. And they did. Stevie later wove her premonition into the 1982 Fleetwood Mac single "Gypsy," which referenced the San Francisco shop, as well as Stevie's consistent personal style, in its lyrics.

"The clothes I wear . . . that doesn't change," she said in 1982 while promoting "Gypsy" and its Fleetwood Mac album, *Mirage*. "I love long dresses. I love velvet. I love high boots. I never change. I love the same eye makeup. I'm not a fad person."

Since launching what is now considered Stevie's trademark look in 1975 (with an assist from the Los Angeles designer Margi Kent, who also curated looks for Christine and Lindsey and other seminal seventies rock musicians), countless magazines and other media have promised to help fans piece together her style with tips for where to source ruffled skirts, fringed shawls, and aviator glasses. But Stevie's fashion influence was—and remains—less about choosing the "correct" accessories to drape across your figure and more about how you subtly ask others to regard you.

In 2013, Stevie sat down for an interview at the annual South by Southwest conference, where she talked about how it felt to join Fleetwood Mac in 1974. For the first time in her adult life, Stevie didn't have to worry about where her next paycheck was coming from, as she and Lindsey had been offered two hundred dollars per week apiece (about a thousand today). After recording Fleetwood Mac's self-titled album in "exactly three months," the band hit the road to tour their new material. "It was (A) a dream job, (B) extremely lucky," Stevie said of that fall spent touring.

Stevie's financial fortunes might have been on the upswing, but she and bandmate Christine McVie understandably felt outnumbered by the "famous rockers" in every room they walked into. "I said to Chris, you know, we can never be treated like second-class citizens here. When we walk into the room, we have to walk in with a big attitude. Which does not mean a snotty, conceited attitude. But it means we have to float in like goddesses, because that is how we want to be treated. And we will never not be invited to the party, because we are women."

Stevie wasn't specifically referring to her fashion sense here, but her style choices did influence how the singer showed up in the world—and at every party—which she and Christine were always invited to after they made that "goddesses" pact. You could think of Stevie's onstage look as a suit of armor—a now timeless blend of romantic femininity and dark, edgy rock 'n' roll. It's a look that she pieced together out of items made to amplify her stage presence, a love of flea markets and antiquing (Stevie famously found her first top hat while antiquing with Christine in Buffalo, New York), and admiration for singers like Janis Joplin and Grace Slick. With her early arsenal of Victorian lace from the markets of Portobello Road, height-boosting platform boots, an endless array of shawls, and volumized, shaggy hair, Stevie could feel confident floating into any room, or onto any stage.

"People will always treat you like a wimp once they have decided that's what you are. . . . You have to be strong and tough and intelligent and smart and kind of plan out what you're going to say and know who you are, so that people will get that right away. Because then they're always going to be great to you. And they're always going to treat you with respect. And that's what you want, because then they listen to you. And then they listen to your songs. And then they give you a chance. Otherwise, you get nowhere."

Thinking of her public look, which Stevie has also described as her "uniform," as a suit of armor was intentional. She also thought of it as a disguise. Initially, she asked Margi to take inspiration from Charles Dickens. Think sheer and raggedy skirts paired with velvet platform boots to elevate her five-foot-one frame. Like a rock 'n' roll Nancy from *Oliver Twist.*

"We came up with the outfit: a Jantzen leotard, a little chiffon wrap blouse, a couple of little short jackets, two skirts, and boots," Stevie said in 2009 of her conversations with Margi. "That gave us our edge. . . . I'll be very, very sexy under eighteen pounds of chiffon and lace and velvet," she continued, touching on her teenage style ideations. "And nobody will know who I really am."

Incorporating shawls into her onstage getup, Stevie realized, also gave her performance a shot of drama, not to mention a practical way for fans seated in the back to get a better view of her (which I can personally confirm, having watched Stevie twirl around in multiple shawls from the second-highest balcony at Brooklyn's massive Barclays Center in late 2025), and a way for her to literally stand up to Mick Fleetwood, who, despite sitting behind his drum kit, could still overwhelm the stage with his towering six-foot-five frame. "A shawl is a great prop. It makes for big gestures. If you want to be seen at the back of that arena, you have to have very big movements."

Stevie drew an equal amount of public fascination for her long, feathered haircut, which she styled in various ways over the years—choppy and layered in the seventies, wild and permed in the eighties, smooth and parted to one side in the nineties. The constant was that she tended to cut and style her hair herself. "If I wasn't a singer, I would have been a hairdresser," she said in 1986. "I wanted to go to hairdressing school, but my parents insisted I go to college to be a second grade teacher, and I turned out a rock 'n' roll singer."

Why would a singer at the top of the charts choose to do her own hair? Again, it was the practical choice. When Fleetwood Mac started touring with Stevie and Lindsey in the seventies, the band simply didn't have anyone helping them with hair styling, so Stevie—no stranger to DIY methods—did it herself. In a backstage video from 1977, Stevie works with her best friend and vocal coach, Robin Anderson, to prep her long, thick hair, asking, "Robin, do we have any bobby pins anywhere?" as she rummages through her bag, tips her head forward, and brushes out the underlayer to build volume. "It's getting fuller by the minute," she cracks.

As Stevie prepared to step away from Fleetwood Mac for the first time in the early 1980s, she evolved her California-girl boho-meets-gothic-gypsy aesthetic into an all-out embrace of white lace. On the cover of *Bella Donna,* Stevie purposely inverted her dark *Rumours* look by wearing an ethereal flowing white gown with long, sheer sleeves that mirrored the white cockatoo (named Max, who belonged to

I'll be very, very
sexy under eighteen
pounds of chiffon
and lace and velvet.
And nobody will
know who I
really am.

her brother) she held aloft. "[As a little girl] I dreamed only about giving a little fairy tale to people," she told *High Times* magazine while promoting her solo debut.

"With my clothes and the things that I wear, I have so much fun. I was talking to a lady today and we were talking about dress-up and about how much fun dress-up used to be. And if there was a trunk in the attic, I was in it looking. And I would rather wear that drape than anything you could sell me from Bloomingdale's. I don't like all that stuff. . . . My fantasy is giving a little bit of the fairy princess to all the people out there that maybe don't have the Hans Christian Andersen books and the Grimm's fairy tales. If that's the only thing I can do for them, well, that's fine."

Stylewise, the more structured 1980s pushed back against the previous two decades. Where loose, feminine blouses and skirts once ruled, the pendulum swung in the opposite direction to square-shouldered power suits, severe and streaky makeup, bright poppy colors, and hairspray-packed perms.

Stevie would continue to play with her style, shifting in the eighties to chunkier jewelry, belts, corset tops, and Southwestern-influenced ponchos, then in the nineties to classic Hollywood gowns, embellished gold shawls, and billowing skirts. Regardless of the decade, however, her style shifts never strayed too far from her original uniform.

"I want to be age-appropriate," she told *WWD* in 2009. "I don't want to be that girl you see walking away and she looks twenty-five and then she turns around and she looks ninety. I don't wear see-through chiffon skirts anymore. I wear a slip. When I was thirty, I didn't care if people could see through my clothes. Now I care."

While Stevie's style reflected each decade's trends, it wouldn't quite be accurate to call it trendy. Stevie tended to put her own spin on of-the-moment cuts, fabrics, and drapes. In the ensuing decades, it wouldn't be unusual for prominent designers to model their designs after Stevie's original wardrobe. A-list celebrities and high-fashion models would also show up at red carpet events decked out in their own boho-gothic interpretation of Stevie's style. Speaking to *The New York Times* about the Stevie-inspired line she designed in the late nineties, Anna Sui said she admired Stevie's consistency. "She's the iconic California woman," Sui said. "Everyone has their version of her."

Part of floating into the room like a goddess involves a sense of genuine self-belief. Wear the clothes, don't let the clothes wear you. Know what you like and what you don't like. Look in unexpected places, like a tiny thrift store in Buffalo, for inspiration. And if all else fails, throw on a top hat for a bit of height.

LESSON SEVEN

DON'T BE SORRY FOR ANYTHING

Everything that was done was meant to be done
in order for us to be sitting here today
with the life that we have.

—Stevie Nicks, Bustle, 2020

I made a promise to myself a long time ago. I would not teach school—I would teach through music. I would try to give a little bit of philosophy through my music and deliver some message to everybody without it being political or without it being taken the wrong way. I can't really think that I would have done it any differently if I had it to do over.

—Stevie Nicks, Off the Record, 2000

Don't misunderstand the title of this chapter. It's important to apologize when you've hurt someone. This is not about refusing to make things right with people you've wronged, but rather about regret. Don't go through life carrying regret for paths not taken or mistakes made. Give yourself some grace for the messes you've made on your way to becoming you.

When asked in 2023 if she had any advice for her twenty-eight-year-old self, Stevie said: "Follow your heart. Because that's exactly what I did. I followed my heart, and I had amazing love affairs—maybe that I shouldn't have had—but my heart said 'Do it,' and I did. I'm not sorry for anything. Everything that was done was meant to be done in order for us to be sitting here today with the life that we have."

We wouldn't have Stevie Nicks—the icon, the rock 'n' roll godmother, the fountain of wisdom—if a young woman named Stephanie Lynn Nicks had not followed her heart straight into the unknown.

Stevie has made a life out of living without regret, arguably since she first begged her parents for guitar lessons as a teenager and certainly when she left home to follow Lindsey Buckingham to Los Angeles. What's interesting in Stevie's 2023 reflection, too, is how she had absolutely zero regrets about her romantic liaisons, many of which were—let's be honest—dramatic.

In November 1977, after releasing *Rumours* with Fleetwood Mac and breaking up for good with Lindsey, Stevie fell into a brief affair with Mick Fleetwood, who was still married to Jenny Boyd—the younger sister of the 1960s model and photographer Pattie Boyd, the first wife of George Harrison. "Never in a million years could you have told me that would happen," Stevie later said in 2012. "Everybody was angry because Mick was married to a wonderful girl and had two wonderful children. I was horrified. I loved these people. I loved his family. So it couldn't possibly work out. And it didn't. I just couldn't." Stevie wasn't exactly single either—almost immediately after breaking up with Lindsey, she'd started to date Don Henley of the Eagles.

Things got messy quickly. Mick confessed the affair to Jenny, who later wrote in her memoir, "At first I didn't understand what he'd said. It took some seconds for it to sink in. I stared at him in silence, feeling as though I'd been kicked in the stomach, my mind and heart in complete turmoil as I struggled to make sense of his words."

Mick and Jenny finally ended their marriage in 1978. But to complicate things further, Mick began to date one of Stevie's best friends, Sara Recor. The two moved in together and were married from 1988 to 1995.

Discussing how hurt she felt while recording Fleetwood Mac's double album *Tusk* in 1979, Stevie said: "Well, here's a big one for ya. I had started to see Mick Fleetwood romantically. I had a very dear friend whose name was Sara, who just went after Mick. And they fell in love, and the next thing, Sara's husband is calling me to say 'Sara moved in with Mick this morning. And I just thought you might wanna know.'

"That was three months into a thirteen-month album. So I lost Mick, which honestly wasn't that big a deal because that was a rocky relationship. But losing my friend Sara? That was a huge blow. Sara was banished from the studio by the rest of the band. . . . No one was speaking, and I wouldn't even look directly at Mick. That went on for months. And it was great fodder for writing! The songs poured out of us."

While Stevie has spoken extensively about following her heart in matters of love and career, she has also mused about forward motion and what it means to be alone on several songs, both solo and with Fleetwood Mac. Take "Silver Springs," another visceral breakup song that has gone on to attain mythical status in the Stevie songbook.

The ultrapersonal midtempo ballad, about the disintegration of her and Lindsey's romantic relationship, was originally meant to appear on *Rumours* but was ultimately cut for time and replaced with the quicker "I Don't Want to Know." Adding insult to injury, the decision to cut "Silver Springs" was made without Stevie's input. (They later released it, but as a non-album B-side to Lindsey's breakup retelling "Go Your Own Way.")

"I was so mad that I started to cry, and I'm pretty sure either I got back in my car and went home, or went in the studio furious and just fumed for eight hours," she told *People* in 2023. "But I didn't get anywhere with that . . . [my] strong woman stance did not really make a difference in that situation at all."

In the fifty years since Stevie wrote "Silver Springs," its stirring refrain has become one of Fleetwood Mac's most enduring, poignant, and recognizable, thanks in part to the band's performing it in 1997 during the taping of a reunion show later released as the Grammy-nominated recording *The Dance*. "Silver Springs" (like "Dreams" and "Landslide") is steeped in duality: While admonishing the person who broke her heart, Stevie casts her gaze to the future. She understands the impossibility of continuing with this man but still allows herself to mourn the loss of a formative romance and ponder what it could have been. At its foundation, however, is the knowledge that she must move on. Living without regret doesn't mean you aren't allowed to ruminate on the past.

Stevie would continue to intertwine themes of heartbreak, following your intuition, and turning the page on solo songs like "Edge of Seventeen," "Wild Heart," and "Leather and Lace." The urgent "Edge of Seventeen," her third single on the debut solo album *Bella Donna,* mourned a different kind of loss—the 1980 assassination of John Lennon and the passing of her uncle shortly afterward, only weeks after he had been diagnosed with cancer. Its iconic, dove-referencing refrain was Stevie's interpretation of the soul leaving its body and a symbol of Lennon and the cause he most stood for: peace.

"That was a very scary and sad moment for all of us in the rock 'n' roll business," Stevie told *Entertainment Weekly* in 2009 of writing "Edge of Seventeen" in the wake of Lennon's assassination. "It scared us all to death that some idiot could be so deranged that he would wait outside your apartment building, never having known you, and shoot you dead."

Meanwhile, "Edge of Seventeen" showed Stevie contemplating her uncle's health decline. "I went home to Phoenix . . . and went to visit my uncle (who was very sick), not knowing that no one but his son, John, was there . . . and I sat on his bedside, while John sat on the floor beside him, and we stayed there. My father did not come, nor my mother . . . nor my aunt . . . so I sat there and held his hand, and sometime right about sunset, he turned his head slightly to John, and then to me, and his hand slowly let go of mine. I did run out into the hallway, but no one was there . . . and the white-winged dove took flight," she recounted in the liner notes to *Timespace: The Best of Stevie Nicks,* her 1991 compilation album.

"The line 'And the days go by like a strand in the wind,' that's how fast those days were going by during my uncle's illness, and it was so upsetting to me," she also told *Rolling Stone* in 1981 while doing press for *Bella Donna.* "The part that says 'I went today . . . maybe I will go again . . . tomorrow' refers to seeing him the day before he died. He was home and my aunt had some music softly playing, and it was a perfect place for the spirit to go away. The white-winged dove in the song is a spirit that is leaving a body, and I felt a great loss at how both Johns were taken. 'I hear the call of the nightbird singing . . . come away . . . come away . . .'"

The dramatic title "Edge of Seventeen" has inspired a lot of coming-of-age moments over the years, such as the 2016 film of the same name starring Hailee Steinfeld, who plays a high school student grappling with the fact that her older brother has started to date her best friend. "Edge of Seventeen" on its face sounds like it's about finding oneself as you prepare to adjust from high school to whatever comes next. In a sense, that's true—after all, the song's theme is change—but change is a lifelong constant, not just a teenage concern.

Around this time in her career, Stevie was going through some extreme change, stepping out on her own for the first time as a solo artist. She'd been spending a lot of time with Tom Petty, who contributed heavily to *Bella Donna,* and Stevie wanted to write a song for him and his then wife, Jane Benyo, who had been high school sweethearts. Suggesting a title for the song, Jane said "At the Age of Seventeen," but Stevie misheard her Southern-drawled "age" as "edge."

The finished product conjoins life and death in a way that gets the listener to take stock of everything they've ever done—or wanted to do—in their own life. There's grief as Stevie processes these dueling deaths but simultaneously entertains the mystical suggestion of rebirth—or at least finding the inner strength to keep looking ahead while resisting the urge to regret what got you to where you are today.

"The energy that was written into that song was so intense that it took us about two nights to get the track to that, and it's like nobody's feet ever stopped moving," Nicks told *Vox* magazine in 1992. "It was like there was this energy that was so strong. I cried in the middle of the bridge thing, about the sea never expects it when it rains, but the sea changes color, but the sea does not change. And so with the slow, graceful flow of age, I went forth with an age-old desire to please. It was like, well, we have to keep going now. And I wanted that song to have all that energy of them and of us going on."

Stevie would face down a mess of regrets as the eighties unfolded into the nineties and the consequences of her rock star life unfolded. While it was important to her that she authentically live a life without regret, she would speak at length about how badly she wished she'd never touched the pharmaceutical Klonopin when it was prescribed to her. "That took eight years out of my life," she said. "Those were my prime years, my forties, when a lot of my heavy creative activity was really happening. Klonopin grabbed hold of you and made you sit down on your couch and not get up. I just watched TV for eight years in a daze. I'm sorry I didn't have a car crash on the way to seeing that doctor."

On the whole, however, Stevie has cemented a habit of channeling any would-be regret right back into her songwriting, which turns out to be a gift for all involved. Of the bass-driven "24 Karat Gold," she told a fan how it was inspired by her doomed relationship with Mick. "Even though it's kind of a sad, crazy song, I'm so glad it all happened so I could write that song," she said. "The '24 karat gold' part was inspired by Mick's beautiful gold jewelry that I had never seen before, and I was so drawn to that yellow gold color, I started collecting pieces of that myself."

Finally, I'd argue that Stevie's greatest regret turned career win was the way she rescued "Silver Springs" from obscurity. In 1997, the classic Fleetwood Mac lineup reunited for their The Dance tour, and one of its shows was filmed and aired on MTV. Not only was "Silver Springs" added to the setlist, but the filmed performance revealed crackling energy between herself and Lindsey, who sang to each other as if the audience did not exist. "When Lindsey and I go back and forth on the songs that were written between the two of us, for that moment, we are back in love again," she said.

After its MTV airing, "Silver Springs" exploded into a Top 40 hit and was nominated for a Grammy in 1998. In 2005, it was added to the remastered *Rumours* edition. It has been a set staple ever since.

I'm so glad it all happened so I could write that song.

LESSON EIGHT

DO SOMETHING CREATIVE EVERY DAY

What a writer wants to do is put stuff out there and make people mull it over in their minds until suddenly it's something that's way more important than turning on the stereo.

—Stevie Nicks, The Island Ear, 1994

Even when Stevie was juggling odd jobs, cleaning gigs, and waitressing, she always left room for creativity. Yes, it was exhausting. But carving out that time to write music every night was in the service of something much bigger.

Also, while reading about this period in her life, you get the sense that writing and singing were things Stevie did not just *want* to do—she felt *compelled* to do them. And then on a practical note, why even commit your life to hustling in Los Angeles—a city packed with creative dreamers—if you don't create just a little bit every day? Even if nothing ever comes of it professionally, or if you never wanted to pursue art as a career, creation itself is therapeutic.

Stevie has certainly maintained as much at different points across her career. In Jenny Boyd's 1992 book *Musicians in Tune: 75 Contemporary Musicians Discuss the Creative Process,* Stevie opened up about her daily ritual with creativity, saying, "Every day I feel I have to do something, whether it's write a paragraph or sit at the piano for five minutes or go to the studio for a little while. If I don't feel I've done something worthwhile every day, then I feel worthless. I feel always that I want to live up to my end of the bargain, that I was given something by God, and He asks only that I give Him back something."

Even as far back as 1981, while promoting *Bella Donna,* Blair Jackson from *BAM* magazine commented on Stevie's growing reputation as a writer. When he asked if she had a writing regimen, she replied that she didn't. "I just write when I feel like it, which is a lot of the time," she said. "Sometimes I write every day, sometimes a few days will go by when I don't write anything. I get nervous that I'm drying up if I don't write often." After musing that her many notebooks contained the complete history of Fleetwood Mac, Stevie said, with her trademark candor: "Writing is fun for me. I've got a wealth of things to write about."

Had it been difficult, Jackson continued, for her to be respected for her craft? To be seen as more than just a "chick singer"?

"I just keep writing, playing, and telling people how important writing is," she replied.

> I tell writers that it's not important to me to be a sex symbol. I tell them it's not important to me what people think of me dancing around in gossamer clothing onstage. I happen to like wearing clothing like that. It's fine for Gelsey Kirkland [a top ballerina] but it's not fine for me. If I was a ballerina, nobody would say one word about what I wore, and they wouldn't talk about my sex life—which writers don't know anything about anyway. But put on a pair of platform boots and walk out on a rock and roll stage and—WOW! All people see is an image.

I'm not going to change because I get criticized for what I wear or because, as you said some people see only a "chick singer." I keep persevering and doing what I do with the hope that someday people won't care about any of that and instead they'll look up and say, "You know, she really is a pretty good writer." It's starting to happen, actually. It's taken six or seven years, but it is happening. You can't give up for a second.

Even in Stevie's less-sparkly moments—like when she was trying to kick Klonopin in the early nineties—she somehow made space for creativity. In 1991, Stevie told *The Denver Post* how she wrote everything down, every day, in a journal. The same year, she spoke to the *Baltimore Sun* about taking some "special time alone," even when she was on the road. "When I see that typewriter when I get in my [hotel] room, it just makes me go, 'Wow.' If I feel like saying anything tonight, it's all there, it's all ready. I light the candles, and I light some incense, and put on some music for whatever mood I'm in, and it's my time."

Just like when she was in her twenties in Los Angeles, Stevie would stay up till all hours just to write something. In the same *Baltimore Sun* interview, Stevie described getting back to her room at around four in the morning after a Fleetwood Mac engagement and sitting at her typewriter for the next three hours. "I was so tired that I would put my head down on the typewriter and almost go to sleep, and then I'd wake back up and I'd type another couple paragraphs," she said. "I go home from every tour with a binder full of journalistic prose of the tour, and then also a lot of poetry. They [the band] don't know that I'm writing this every night, I don't show them until the end of the tour. Then I have it bound into a little book, and I give it to everybody."

Of course, not everyone is built to keep late hours. I include myself in that camp; I get my best writing done early in the morning, and I'm a zombie by nine at night. If I'm being completely honest, I'm pretty useless most days by midafternoon. But it's not so much about *when* you do something creative so much as it is about finding just a little time to carve out each day. Maybe it's in the early morning, before the kids wake up. Maybe it's in the evening, after they go to sleep. Maybe it's during your lunch break. Maybe you don't have kids or are now an empty nester. Simply dedicating a few minutes to an hour of creative time each day adds up, sort of like saving a few dollars here and there for a future vacation.

Maybe you don't even regard yourself as being creative. I can't begin to tell you how many people have approached me over the years telling me how they could *never* be a writer. What would they even say? But I'm a firm believer in the fact that everyone has creativity within themselves. Take it from Stevie, who gave this advice in 1992 about keeping a journal to build a writing habit:

I tell people all the time that they should keep a journal, even if it's just "I had a terrible day today and I don't want to talk about it, love, Stevie," or "I dreamt last night . . ." Even if it's just three sentences, because at the end of five or six days, you would have created a habit, and you will find that over a month that you have a whole story growing. Whether it's just for your own memories, so you can go back at any age, or if you are a writer or a singer, or some part of the creative business, you can be creative. Anyone can be creative if they want to—you just have to want to.

Creativity can also spark from the most unusual places. It's a bit of a misconception that creative types are constantly puttering around the house, mulling over massive concepts. I mean, perhaps some of us are, but frankly, that sounds exhausting. In reality, ideas tend to show up suddenly, often out of mundane moments. Stevie, who is always attempting to see beyond the veil, once spoke about simply paying close attention to her feelings and developing creative ideas from there. It sounds so easy—just pay attention to your feelings!—but you'd probably be amazed at how many people go through day-to-day life never once looking within. Like art or writing, just a little bit each day can add up to immense perspective and self-understanding.

"Pay attention to your feelings," Stevie said of her creative process in 1992. "It can be anything. Everything. And yes, I can write a really super romantic song today even though I'm not really in a relationship nor have I been in one for a long time. I can take ideas right out of the air, but I have to be really inspired. It has to be something truly inspiring that pushes me to go and write a poem, and then that poem is something that, when I have the time, I will take to the piano. That has always been my process since I was fifteen years old."

Stevie has been remarkably consistent in her descriptions of sparking creativity. In 2007, Reprise Records released *Crystal Visions—The Very Best of Stevie Nicks,* a compilation containing some hit singles, a dance remix, one new song, and a live version of Led Zeppelin's "Rock and Roll." While promoting that project, Stevie sat down on *CBS Sunday Morning* and broke down her songwriting process, step by step.

First, she'll see something. Next, a tiny detail becomes a line. The line starts a poem. Stevie takes the poem to a piano. "It just starts with a little inspiration. Something will happen . . . whether it happens to me, whether it happens to a man who walks by me and smiles a certain way, that just makes me go, 'What a beautiful smile that was.' Then I just might go and write, 'The smile was the only thing I saw . . .' Then my poem has begun."

Pay attention to your feelings. It can be anything. Everything. And yes, I can write a really super romantic song today even though I'm not really in a relationship nor have I been in one for a long time. I can take ideas right out of the air, but I have to be really inspired.

LESSON NINE

LOOK TO YOUR GUARDIAN ANGELS

Again I say, I wish the guardian angels to stand at your side. I wish that you remain safe.

—Stevie Nicks's letter to armed forces servicemembers on Thanksgiving Eve, 2004

I grew up in the 1990s—a very popular time for angels. You had the TV show *Touched by an Angel,* the ABC sitcom *Teen Angel,* Kevin Smith's *Dogma. Buffy the Vampire Slayer* had a bloodsucking boyfriend called Angel; every piece of teen-girl clothing seemed to feature a halo or wings on the back or butt. I even loved to reread a YA trilogy called *Kissed by an Angel,* in which a teenager's boyfriend dies but comes back to protect her from his killer. (Kind of like *Ghost* for the YA set.)

Stevie has a similar (albeit far less trendy) interest in guardian angels, and it's something she's talked about frequently. On her shimmering 1989 track "Ghosts," which appeared on her fourth solo album, *The Other Side of the Mirror,* Stevie addressed her tendency to ruminate over the past while suggesting that her guardian angel might encourage her to think of her past, present, and future in a less linear fashion. Could it be that time isn't chronological, the way we imagine it to be on earth? But instead, it's all happening simultaneously? In the philosophy of space and time, that's a real concept called "eternalism," and it's one Stevie seemed to address when talking about "Ghosts" in 1989.

"We all turn to our guardian angels at some point . . . I truly believe that guardian angels are out there, and I believe that we've all got one sitting on our shoulder. . . . 'Ghosts' for me . . . at the end becomes somewhat . . . I don't want even to use the word 'holy,' but there is certainly a spiritual thing about it, you know, and you turn to your guardian angel, and you realize that the ghosts of the past and the present and the future all are a part of you and that you have to dig the past and the future and what you're living day to day and you have to stop for a second and check out how cool today is and how cool yesterday was and also hopefully how cool tomorrow's gonna be."

Across the whole of her life, Stevie has been unabashedly spiritual. Calling Stevie "spiritual" is not to say she is traditionally religious (unless you count her diehard fans adopting her 2024 declaration to *Rolling Stone:* "I believe in the Church of Stevie"). In 1998, in an interview promoting her *Enchanted* box set, Stevie described her unconventional outlook on God to *Billboard* magazine: "I am religious. I wasn't raised in any religion, because we were always moving when I was a kid and didn't get involved in any church. But I believe there have been angels with me constantly through these last twenty years, or I wouldn't be alive."

During the same *Enchanted* promotion cycle, Stevie again acknowledged her belief in an all-knowing entity, reasoning that she couldn't have survived the hardships she'd faced in life alone while jokingly attributing her youthful appearance in middle age to a divine being. "I think there is definitely a God. I think there was definitely an angel with me all the way through the bad times. Somebody keeping me safe. I feel very spiritual now. I really believe that God makes my music good and makes me able to deliver it and makes me able to not look or feel fifty. I mean, there has to be some outside help—this can't all be happening on its own."

Stevie has also spoken about an ongoing spiritual connection to her late mother, Barbara, who died suddenly of emphysema and pneumonia in December 2011. The two were remarkably close. "My mother was always totally supportive of me and whatever I wanted to do, even as a young girl," she said in *Oprah's Master Class.* "She wanted me to be fearless . . . She continually was telling me all of her little wise ways to get through life."

Barbara Nicks preferred to keep Stevie close when she was young, telling her daughter how important it was to retain financial independence as a woman, and particularly as a married woman. "She said to me: 'You will never stand in a room full of men and feel like you can't keep up with them. And you will never depend upon a man to support you.' She drummed that into me, and I'm so glad she did."

While Stevie mourned the loss of her mother, she opened up about continuing to feel her presence at unexpected moments, telling *The Guardian* in 2020: "Some people are really afraid of dying, but I'm not. I've always believed in spiritual forces. I absolutely know that my mom is around all the time." In 2012, shortly after her mother's death, Stevie was standing in her kitchen with "really bad acid reflux . . . And I felt something almost tap my shoulder and this voice go: 'It's that Gatorade you're drinking.' I'd been sick and chugging down the Hawaiian Punch. Now, that's not some romantic, gothic story of your mother coming back to you. It's your real mother, walking into your kitchen and saying 'Don't drink any more of that shit.'"

In 2020, Stevie spoke to the *Los Angeles Times* about feeling that a psychic connection to spirits had materialized following her mother's death. "If she can't find something—an errant earring, a pack of matches, a book of poetry—she voices the item aloud and her mom helps her find it," wrote Amy Kaufman. "It's so real and creepy," Stevie continued, "and I always just go 'Thank you, Barbara.' I sometimes feel I have more of a relationship with my mom since she's been dead than I did before she died."

In other instances, Stevie has repeatedly talked about feeling the presence of deceased friends and musicians like Fleetwood Mac singer/keyboardist Christine McVie (who died in 2022 of a stroke amid a cancer battle), Tom Petty, and Prince. We'll dig deeper into these foundational friendships a little later. For now, let's look at how Stevie has surrounded herself with spirits.

Following Christine's passing, Stevie began wearing

a pendant containing some of the ashes of her friend, whom she'd referred to often as her "musical soulmate" over the years. While performing "Landslide" during solo shows, Stevie would feature photomontages of the Fleetwood Mac keyboardist. She felt unable to look at them, though, because she would become overwhelmed with emotion. "She's gone, but she's not gone," Stevie said in 2025. "She's with me a lot. I feel her presence all the time, especially onstage. She's here."

Meanwhile, Stevie took the death of her good friend and collaborator Tom Petty particularly hard. The '70s rock guitar great and leader of the Heartbreakers, who died suddenly in 2017 of an accidental overdose of prescription medication, had been instrumental in inspiring Stevie's first solo album away from Fleetwood Mac, *Bella Donna,* which featured their duet "Stop Draggin' My Heart Around."

In January 2018, Stevie gave a speech about Petty at the Recording Academy's MusiCares Person of the Year event honoring Fleetwood Mac at Radio City Music Hall in New York City. "The loss of Tom Petty has just about broken my heart," Stevie told the audience. "He was not only a good man to go down the river with, as Johnny Cash said, he was a great father, and he was a great friend. He was one of my best friends. My heart will never get over this."

Like channeling the spirit of Christine McVie onstage, Stevie regularly thinks about Tom Petty and Prince (the "When Doves Cry" singer died of an accidental fentanyl overdose in 2016) when she's getting ready to perform. In 2020,

If I have a really big,
important show,
I call in all my
spirits, and I say,
"Tom, stand behind
me. Prince, stand
with me."

while promoting her 24 Karat Gold concert special, she talked to *Variety* about reaching out to Tom and Prince's spirits. "If I have a really big, important show, I call in all my spirits, and I say, 'Tom, stand behind me. Prince, stand with me.'"

She continued of Prince, whom she first met in 1983 at a cocktail party: "The Prince thing started a long time ago, because sometimes even before Prince died, I would say that I wish Prince was here and he could just walk with me out there; because of his performing ability and how good he was onstage, sometimes I'd just go, 'Come with me.'"

Even if you don't believe in the literal presence of spirits or angels, even if anything spiritual sounds overly "woo-woo," thinking about the people you love who have passed on can be an enormous comfort, particularly in scary or anxious times. By the same token, thinking of those we love who have passed on can be a tremendous source of inspiration.

If you take nothing else away from this chapter, however, let it be something Stevie once said about taking advantage of the time you have left with the people you love—you never know when it'll be cut short. Shortly after Barbara died, Stevie talked about how her mother's death was so sudden that she was shocked. Stevie thought she'd have years left with her mother, who was eighty-four when she died, Stevie thought she would have so much more time to ask her mother about her life. "I thought I had years left to ask her all those questions that I wanted to ask her. Then she was gone, and I didn't get to. It wasn't because I didn't want to sit down with her and talk to her about her life. It was just because I didn't think she was going anywhere."

The sudden loss of her mother served as an important lesson to Stevie—one she has since passed on to her fans and followers. It's a simple one: Take advantage of the time you have left with your loved ones. "My advice to everybody that still has their parents is, make sure that you sit down and talk to them about what they did when they were kids and what they were like when they were young and when they were first married. All those things. Because you really lose out if you don't. Time waits for no one, and things can end tomorrow. So, if there's stuff you want to know, find out."

LESSON TEN

BE A TOTALLY FREE WOMAN

People say, "But you're alone." But I don't feel alone. I feel very un-alone. I feel very sparkly and excited about everything.

—Stevie Nicks, Vulture, 2013

Although she is a self-proclaimed romantic, Stevie has lived most of her life unmarried and child-free. Her reasoning for these life choices is pretty uncomplicated; opting out of marriage and motherhood has simply allowed Stevie to prioritize herself, her choices, and her career ambitions. While she has spoken fondly and matter-of-factly about these decisions, she has never directly advised anyone else not to get married, stay single, or not have children. She has only ever known what is right for herself, and that kind of self-knowledge is rare—and admirable.

"I'm single, I don't have children, and I've never been married except for three months a long time ago," Stevie said in 2014. "It wasn't a marriage of reality. I live a single woman's life and yes, I spend a lot of time by myself. I have a few very close friends, most of them I've known forever, and I kind of like it. Would I be willing to have a boyfriend? It would be fun if I could find a boyfriend who understood my life and didn't get his feelings hurt because I'm always a phone call away from having to leave in two hours for New York or a phone call away from having to do interviews all day long. It's not very much fun to be Mr. Stevie Nicks. In the last ten years I've just said I'm going to follow my muse. If I want to go somewhere I don't have to worry about anyone being mad at me. I don't have to make up excuses on the phone about why I'm not coming home."

Given Stevie and Lindsey's formative relationship, one would imagine that they'd have tried marriage at some point. Stevie has theorized that they might have gotten married and had kids if they'd never joined Fleetwood Mac. "Lindsey always blamed Fleetwood Mac for the loss of me," she said in 2013. "Had we not joined Fleetwood Mac, we would have continued with our music, we probably would have gotten married, we probably would have had a child, and it would have been a different life. . . . We were still young enough then that destiny could have taken us another way, but destiny did not take us that way."

Stevie's decision not to become a mother was tested in 1977. When she became unexpectedly pregnant by then boyfriend Don Henley of the Eagles, she briefly considered what life might look like with a baby. When she told Don about the baby, who she thought would be a girl named Sara, Don sounded excited. But he appeared to change his mind about the prospect and grew distant. As Don's attention wavered, Stevie made the tough decision to end the pregnancy. It was the right one for her, and as she has pointed out, the right call for Fleetwood Mac, which would have been "done" if she'd gone ahead with the pregnancy.

"Don was the first guy I actually went out with after Lindsey and I broke up," Stevie later told *Rolling Stone* in 2024. "When this pregnancy happened, it was like, 'What the heck happened? I am completely respectful of the world rules here, and all of a sudden this happens to me, and I can't figure it out.' I go to my GYN, and he says, 'Well, you've been protected by your Copper-7 IUD, but you have a tipped uterus. That IUD is only protecting half of you, and we didn't know that.'

"Now what the hell am I going to do? I cannot have a child. I am not the kind of woman who would hand my baby over to a nanny, not in a million years. So we would be dragging a baby around the world on tour, and I wouldn't do that to my baby. I wouldn't say I just need nine months. I would say I need a couple of years, and that would break up the band, period. So my decision was to have an abortion. If people want to be mad at me about that, I don't really care, because my life was my life, and my plan was my plan and had been since I was in the fourth grade."

Awkwardly, Don would reveal Stevie's abortion to the public in a 1991 interview with *GQ* in which he told the magazine how he thought Fleetwood Mac's *Tusk* track "Sara" was about their short-lived relationship. "I believe, to the best of my knowledge, she became pregnant by me," he said. "And she named the kid Sara, and she had an abortion and then wrote the song of the same name to the spirit of the aborted baby." (In response, Stevie had one retort: "He wishes!")

Despite everything, the pair remained good friends; Don appeared on Stevie's *Bella Donna* single "Leather and Lace," and in 1994 Stevie admitted that Don had partially (if not entirely) inspired "Sara," which was more about "a very good friend of mine whose name is Sara [Recor], who was married to Mick Fleetwood. She likes to think it's completely about her, but it's really not completely about her. It's about me, about her, about Mick, about Fleetwood Mac. It's about all of us at that point. There's little bits about each one of us in that song, and when it had all the other verses, it really covered a vast bunch of people."

Just as Stevie was tested in her decision not to become a mother, fate tested her resolve not to be anyone's wife a few times over the years. Stevie was married once, in the early 1980s, to her best friend's widower, Kim Anderson. Theirs was a marriage born of grief and lasted only three months. "It was a terrible, terrible mistake," she said in 1990. "We didn't get married because we were in love, we got married because we were grieving, and it was the only way that we could feel like we were doing anything."

One of Stevie's oldest friends, Robin Ann Snyder met the singer when they were fifteen at Arcadia High School. When Stevie started touring with Fleetwood Mac, Robin would be on hand backstage with Stevie to assist with hair and makeup. "Robin was one of those people [who] when she walked in the room everybody looked," Stevie told *The Arizona Republic* in 1983, the same year she dedicated her *Wild Heart* song "Nightbird" to Robin.

In 1981, Robin was diagnosed with leukemia. About two

months later, when she was in remission, Robin became pregnant. Her remission did not last; the leukemia returned. But Robin opted against terminating the pregnancy, which would have allowed for her illness to be treated more aggressively. The disease progressed rapidly, and doctors were forced to deliver Robin and Kim's son, Matthew, prematurely, at just over six months. Robin died only days later. Stevie took her friend's death hard. "I just went crazy," she said. "I just went insane. And so did her husband. And we were the only two that could really understand the depth of the grief that we were going through. And I was determined to take care of that baby, so I said to Kim, 'I don't know, I guess we should just get married.'"

The couple's friends and families met this news with a mixture of confusion and anger. Only Stevie's mother and brother attended the 1983 nuptials, as did Mick and Christine McVie. "I could see on her face that she knew it was a mistake," Mick later related in *Gold Dust Woman*.

Part of Stevie's motivation for marrying Kim Anderson was so she could be the one to care for Matthew, Robin and Kim's new baby. "I thought that's what Robin would want, but it just blew up in our faces."

Things fell apart quickly. Kim began to complain that Stevie, who was working on *Bella Donna,* was spending too much time in the studio and not enough time with him and Matthew. Meanwhile, Stevie realized the absurdity of marrying Kim one day when she walked into Matthew's room and didn't see the cradle rocking. It had always been rocking slightly before, which Stevie took as a sign that Robin was there with them. Stevie took something away from that moment, where Matthew's cradle lay still. "She's gone," she said to baby Matthew, before walking upstairs and waiting for Kim to come home. "I don't love you, and you don't love me. You may think you love me, but you don't," she told Kim, whom she advised to move back to Minnesota, where he was from. "Kim, I'm a rock and roll star. It's what I do. It's who I am."

Even in that low moment, Stevie understood why marrying Kim felt like the right decision at the time, and why staying married was ultimately not an option. For one, she did not love Kim; their shared grief had brought them together to create a false imitation of love. For another, Stevie knew her priorities. "I made a choice years ago not to ever be married and not to have children, because it would get in the way of being a true artist and following my true calling, which is being the artist that I am now."

By now, maybe you've noticed a pattern involving the way Stevie expresses herself and decides her life: Every choice is a combination of in-the-clouds spirituality and down-to-earth pragmatism. When it came to marriage and motherhood, Stevie made it clear to anyone who asked that her art and music came first; for her, being an artist was ultimately incompatible with marriage, which asks you to prioritize your spouse.

After the dissolution of her marriage to Kim, Stevie went years without speaking to him or Matthew. "I suppose that Matthew will find me when he's ready. I mean, I am, really, next to Robin, his mommy," she said in 1990. "But Kim and I can't deal with each other at all. So, when the baby's old enough, I have all of his mother's things, and I have her life on film for fourteen, fifteen years. I have us on tape singing, I have a beautiful book that I wrote the year that she died. . . . I have a roomful of stuff for him. I have his mother to give back to him when he's ready."

Happily, Stevie did reunite with Matthew Anderson when he got older; she even paid for his college education. Today, Matthew has a daughter named Robin, after his mother, and she calls Stevie "Grandma Stevie." "On that day I wrote in my journal, 'I promise you, Robin, that I will be Grandma Stevie until death does us part.'"

Stevie again came close to marriage a few years later when she fell into a passionate relationship with Eagles singer and guitarist Joe Walsh, who opened for her Wild Heart tour in 1983. When the two met at the Mansions Hotel in Dallas in 1983, it was love at first sight. "I looked at him and I walked across the room and I sat on the bar stool next to him, and two seconds later I crawled into his lap, and that was it," she later told *The Telegraph*. "I remember thinking, 'I can never be far from this person again.'" (One hiccup: Joe was still on his third marriage, to Juanita Boyer.)

But both stars were dealing with myriad personal issues,

which weighed on their relationship and ultimately made it impossible to go the distance. Stevie, still reeling from losing Robin, was heavily addicted to cocaine. Joe, also struggling with addiction, was still dealing with grief over the loss of his baby daughter Emma, who died in 1973 in a car accident. (He would later chronicle this loss in his solo "Song for Emma.")

"He seemed to be in a lot of pain, though he hid it well," Stevie later wrote in the liner notes for her 1991 retrospective album *Timespace,* which also described a road trip the pair took to the "snow-covered hills" of Colorado in September 1983. After a concert in Denver, Stevie had been complaining about some of the conditions on their tour, and Joe responded by asking her to go for a ride with him, two hours north to Boulder. "He wouldn't tell me where we were going. . . . But he did tell me a story of a little daughter that he had lost. . . . I guess I had been complaining about a lot of things going on on the road, and he decided to make me aware of how unimportant my problems were, compared to worse sorrows. So, he told me that he had taken his little girl to this magic park whenever he could, and the only thing she ever complained about was that she was too little to reach up to the drinking fountain.

"As we drove up to this beautiful park [North Boulder Park] (it was snowing a little bit), he came around to open my door and help me down, and when I looked up and saw the park . . . his baby's park, I burst into tears, saying, 'You built a

In the last ten years I've just said I'm going to follow my muse. If I want to go somewhere I don't have to worry about anyone being mad at me. I don't have to make up excuses on the phone about why I'm not coming home.

drinking fountain here for her . . . didn't you?' I was right, under a huge, beautiful hanging tree was a tiny silver drinking fountain, . . . I left Joe to get to it, and on it it said, 'Dedicated to HER and all others who were too small to get a drink.'"

Once back home in Phoenix, Stevie sat down at her piano and wrote "Has Anyone Ever Written Anything for You," which she dedicated to Joe. "Thank you, Joe, for the most committed song I ever wrote," she continued in the liner notes. "But more than that, thank you for inspiring me in so many ways. Nothing in my life ever seems as dark anymore since we took that drive."

For Stevie, Joe was The One. She contemplated marrying him. "We were probably the perfect, complete, crazy pair," she said. "He was the one I would have married, and that I would probably have changed my life around for . . . a little bit, anyway. Not a lot. But he wouldn't have changed his life either."

But there were problems emblematic of rock stars dating rock stars. For starters, Stevie and Joe were both using—and heavily addicted to—cocaine. Stevie also felt neglected and ignored by the Eagle, seeming always to be waiting around to get a moment alone with him. The breaking point came in 1986 when Joe came to visit her in the studio—except he spent most of the studio session getting high and hanging out with the studio crew before telling her he was actually leaving the next day to tour. That was it. Stevie was done.

"It nearly killed me," she later said. "We had to break up, or we thought we'd die. We were just too excessive. But there was no closure. It took me years to get over it—if I ever did. But at least we survived."

Opening up to the singer Sheryl Crow, Stevie also reminisced once about how "I look back at all the men in my life, and there was only one that I can honestly say I could have lived with every day for the rest of my life, because there was respect and we loved to do the same things. I was very content with him all the time. That's only happened once in my life. The point is, it can happen—this kind of love. This man, if he'd asked me to marry him, I would have."

The music world got some classic breakup ballads out of Stevie and Joe's separation. Stevie's good friend Tom Petty allegedly titled 1985's "Don't Come Around Here No More" based on a fight Stevie and Joe had during which Stevie threw out the titular phrase. (At least, that's according to the Eurythmics' Dave Stewart, who co-wrote the Petty single and claimed to have witnessed the fight after a party at Stevie's.) Fun fact: "Don't Come Around Here No More" was almost on Stevie's 1985 solo album *Rock a Little,* but after Stevie heard Petty sing it, she felt the song belonged more to him.

Ironically, Stevie never released any songs (that we know of—there's still time) directly about Joe other than "Has Anyone Ever Written Anything for You." She has, however, doubled down on her wish never to be married or a mother. Her unique position in the world brought up something of a catch-22: Stevie understood, on an intellectual level, how marriage could complicate her ambition. Especially a marriage to a fellow rock star. On the flip side, only another rock star could understand a chaotic life of touring and unpredictability.

Stevie told *Us* magazine in 1990, "I mean, everybody that I've ever gone with in my life—rich rock and roll stars, poor guys that didn't have a penny, guys in completely other businesses—they finally just look at me and say, 'I really love you, and if you were ever around, that would continue. But I don't ever get to see you,

and I can't dig the way that you live. I can't deal with the jealousy, I can't deal with the fact that the whole world seems to be more important to you than I am.' I've had many really wonderful relationships, but they always seem to end up in that bag. That's the saddest part for me, I think."

Contrary to the have-it-all feminist narrative once popularized by *Cosmopolitan* editor Helen Gurley Brown, Stevie took a highly realistic view of her ambitions and concluded, after some trial and error, that the type of icon status she craved just didn't provide space for husbands and children. "I made a choice to not be married and not have children, because I wanted to be a big-time rock and roll star," she told *Rolling Stone*. "And people can get mad at me for saying this, but I did not feel that I could do both. I would have been, I think, a great mom, and I would not have put my career first once I had a baby. . . . Even in my really bad, drugged-out days, I didn't go away. I still toured, still did interviews. I never gave up the fight. That's why I'm who I am today, because I didn't leave. And I think I made the right choice."

Stevie's periodic questioning of her choices only emphasizes her candor and humanity. Reading over her interviews, particularly in the *Bella Donna* era, you can hear Stevie debating with herself (or a journalist) what kind of love would be powerful enough to bring her to choose a traditional family life. While she has been consistent in her decision not to marry or be a mother over the decades, there have been plenty of moments when she mourned the more anonymous life she might have had, one that could have included domesticity.

"You cannot call in sick to Fleetwood Mac," Stevie told *Playboy* in 1982.

> So a certain number of my relationships are ruined, not because of the people involved but because of my other commitments. And so, every time, I'm just a little less interested in starting something up, because what has happened before is probably going to happen again. It's not a lack of interest on my part; it's a lack of time to be interested.
>
> So maybe it's good that I haven't fallen deeply enough in love to give up a good half of what I do. I wouldn't

want to be a bad mother. And how could I be a good one when I don't even have time to go to the dentist? So forget the child. And forget the boyfriend. I have so many commitments that he would have to come fourth—and I don't like making anybody feel he's fourth.

But, the reporter pushed back, love is clearly very important to you. "Yeah, but I'm at the point where I realize that if my job is what I want to be doing, I'd just better stay out of the sea [of love]," she replied. "I've been going with someone since I was eighteen years old. I think I had a month between Lindsey [Buckingham] and Don [Henley, of the Eagles]. There has always been someone in my life. And I want my freedom at this point, because I really need to get to know Stevie again. I need to be able to paint all night without making someone feel horrible because he's waiting for me to come to bed."

"She told me that she has sacrificed her personal contentment for her career," remembered *Uncut* magazine's Nigel Williamson in *Stevie Nicks: Through the Looking Glass*. "And I think she felt that quite strongly, and it comes out in some of the songs. There is this dichotomy between the life she might have had and the life that she has had. I then asked her what she would change, and the answer was, 'Very little if anything.'"

Regardless of the relationships floating through her life and music, Stevie has generally always circled back to herself.

Not in a self-absorbed way, but in an unwillingness to sacrifice her personal freedom and happiness. Chatting with *The Guardian* in 2020, Stevie shed some new light on "Storms," candidly saying, "Oh, that one was a—excuse my language—'fuck you' to Mick. . . . I sat at my piano, a feminist woman, and I wrote it, to say that nothing you or anybody else can do to me can change the fact that, as the opening line goes: 'Every night that goes between / I feel a little less.'" The song is about freedom, she says. "I am a totally free woman, and I am independent, and that's exactly what I always wanted to be."

Stevie is just one person, and her choice to remain single and childfree need not apply to everyone. Legions of famous performers—and lesser-known but still influential names—have opted in to marriage, partnership, and/or parenthood. What's more, plenty of people decide not to have children or pursue a high-profile career. (It does not have to be one or the other.) There is no "right" choice—only what you choose for yourself. All Stevie would ask you to do is know what that choice is and be unafraid to make it.

I am a totally free
woman, and I am
independent,
and that's exactly
what I always
wanted to be.

LESSON ELEVEN

NEVER STOP BEING A ROMANTIC

I don't fall in love that often, because it's sad when you fall in love and it doesn't work out. I know it's better to have loved, because otherwise I wouldn't have anything to write about. And there are different kinds of love.

—Stevie Nicks, Playboy, 1982

I can sit down at the piano and take out a poem that I wrote right in the middle of a really great relationship and make it into a song. Right now, at seventy-two years old. So when people say, "Can you still write romantic songs?"
I absolutely can.

—Stevie Nicks, Los Angeles Times, 2020

Stevie may have been married only once, for three months and absolutely for the wrong reasons, but that has never stopped her from being the ultimate romantic. Her sentimentalist side showed up as early as "I've Loved and I've Lost," which, recall, she wrote at just sixteen. Only a true believer in romance could write songs like "Beautiful Child" (rumored to be about Beatles manager Derek Taylor, with whom Stevie had a dalliance), "Crystal," "Dreams," "Blue Denim," "Beauty and the Beast," and the all-consuming "Silver Springs."

In fact, Stevie is a romantic in the purest sense of the word. Stevie's own artistry and aesthetic are wrapped up in the philosophical tenets of the artistic movement called Romanticism. Arising in response to the reason-oriented Enlightenment era, Romanticism materialized after the French Revolution of 1789 and placed value in great passion and in exploration of behavioral and emotional states. "Romanticism is precisely situated neither in choice of subject nor in exact truth, but in a way of feeling," wrote the poet and critic Charles Baudelaire in 1846—a hundred years before Stevie would be born, but Baudelaire might well have been describing Stevie.

"If you stop being a romantic, you stop being a poet," Stevie said in 2016. "It's very sad—once you stop being a romantic, you can no longer be a poet. If you are, you're a lousy poet and nobody's going to want to read your poems because they're just jaded and miserable. If you can't write something that's going to inspire people, they're not going to read it. They're going to look at your work and then they're going to say, 'This person is done. That career is over.'"

While Stevie might have been enough of a romantic to seriously consider marriage, marriage as an institution wasn't always enough to keep her romantic feelings at bay. Let's go back to Mick Fleetwood, who was technically married to Jenny Boyd when he and Stevie fell for each other in late 1977 just before Fleetwood Mac left LA for the New Zealand, Japan, and Australia leg of the band's Rumours tour. Mick and Jenny had been married for seven years. Jenny had previously had an affair with guitarist Bob Weston, who'd played in Fleetwood Mac until the early seventies.

Mick was no saint either; the lanky, charming drummer had a bit of a playboy reputation. Mick was taken with Stevie from the moment he first saw her at Sound City with Lindsey. At first, Mick would sneak away from his shared LA home with Jenny to go spend time with Stevie, and the two would go on long drives together up and down Mulholland Drive. As Fleetwood Mac started the tour, close quarters and ample alcohol and drugs meant that the two were thrown together even more. Their affair took on a more torrid quality, too, considering how much sneaking around they were doing, not wanting to upset (a) Jenny, (b) the rest of the band, or (c) Lindsey.

In Stephen Davis's *Gold Dust Woman,* the author describes the scenic drives Mick would take with Stevie around Wellington, New Zealand, where they were chauffeured "through mountain ridges and valleys. It was spring in the Antipodes, and the windows of the Daimler limousine allowed fresh air into the dark cabin where Stevie sat holding hands with Mick Fleetwood, breathing. When they arrived at a famous lookout point just before dawn, they got out and strolled along a deer path, waiting for the sun to break through the clouds overlooking a vast, greening landscape." Pretty crazy romantic, right? It's the stuff of fantasies.

In another stolen moment, Mick swept Stevie up for a kiss behind the stage curtain after a performance in Sydney. Never mind that Jenny was standing only a few inches away, but hey, romance is romance, and Stevie never forgot that smooch, which she later said was one of the most romantic of her life.

Mick and Stevie's romance, which Stevie called "the biggest surprise," was about seeking comfort. In addition to managing Fleetwood Mac, Mick's marriage to Jenny was on the rocks; he'd been diagnosed with hypoglycemia and was self-medicating; and his father had been diagnosed with cancer. "Mick and I never would have had an affair if we hadn't been . . . coked out," Stevie later told Oprah Winfrey.

As ill-advised as their coupling was at the time (if only for its effect on the band), Stevie never lost her respect for Mick, whom she wrote many songs about and still performs with in Fleetwood Mac. But by 1979, Stevie had written a handful of songs about Mick, a few of which made it onto the more experimental *Tusk*.

In the *Tusk* liner notes, Stevie wrote of the stripped-down and contemplative "Storms": "Here's that song in a nutshell: Don't break up other people's marriages. It will never work and will haunt you for the rest of your miserable days."

Another now classic *Tusk* song Stevie wrote to process the Mick situation was "Sara," the very same "Sara" that Don Henley thought was about his and Stevie's unborn child. While Stevie has since admitted that pieces of "Sara" were kind-of-maybe-a-little about Don, the "Sara" in question was much more centered on Sara Recor, Stevie's good friend who also fell for Mick. Though Stevie and Mick were never officially a couple—their relationship was more on-again, off-again—Stevie was nonetheless devastated when he began seeing Sara. (The two eventually married in 1988.)

Stevie dug back into her relationship with Mick on the gently waltzing "Beauty and the Beast," which appeared on *The Wild Heart*. "It was definitely about Mick, . . . but it's also based on the 1946 Jean Cocteau movie," she later told *Entertainment Weekly*. "I first saw it on TV one night when Mick and I were first together, and I always thought of Mick

Don't break up other people's marriages. It will never work and will haunt you for the rest of your miserable days.

as being sort of Beauty and the Beastesque, because he's so tall and he had beautiful coats down to here, and clothes made by little fairies up in the attic, I always thought, so he was that character in a lot of ways. . . . And also, it matched our story because Mick and I could never be, (A) because Mick was married and then divorced and that was not good, and (B) because of Fleetwood Mac."

Just as they pulled from multiple moments and inspirations, Stevie's love songs also tended to be nonlinear. In 1994, Stevie released the rollicking Mike Campbell (of the Heartbreakers) co-write "Blue Denim" about a nameless lover's piercing blue eyes. "It's a song about this guy who came into my life but left just as quick. And his eyes were that intense, that it just makes you, even if you didn't know him, you would go, like, 'wow.' And you could be, like, the toughest person, but those eyes would make you be whatever he wanted you to be." However, it wasn't very long before Stevie completely demystified the subject of "Blue Denim," whom she revealed to be her ex-boyfriend and bandmate Lindsey Buckingham.

Whether they were short-term flings, an on-off affair, or a coupledom lasting years, Stevie poured her personal experiences with love into her songs. Even when writing a breakup anthem like "Silver Springs," Stevie's belief in love and romance rises to the surface. (Why else would she keep falling if she didn't continue to carry a torch for love itself?)

Not content to have her protagonists ride off into the sunset, Stevie tends to tell the full story in her love songs, which capture the stratospheric highs and resultant lows. A song like "Love Is" (the final track on 2001's *Trouble in Shangri-La*), which Stevie wrote with Sarah McLachlan, describes a blissful, hidden romance, which leads to a world of pain when it inevitably ends.

Torrid love connections pop up again and again across Stevie's writing. On 2011's *In Your Dreams,* which the singer co-wrote with her old pal Dave Stewart from Eurythmics, the lead single, "Secret Love," tells the story of a clandestine affair. Stevie wrote "Secret Love" in the midseventies, just after her breakup with Lindsey. Ironically, Stevie said she couldn't remember who it was about.

"I have really tried to remember who it was about," Nicks said. "But at the end of 1975, the world was spinning around us so fast, and we were meeting people every other day. There were gorgeous men and gorgeous women everywhere. We were fast and beautiful and crazy. . . . It must have been secret because I wrote it, recorded it and put it in a box." The "who" behind "Secret Love" wasn't important. Stevie captured not a person but a feeling.

"Crystal" is another long look at enduring love and the "crystalline knowledge" it offers. First appearing on *Buckingham Nicks,* the delicate "Crystal" got repurposed for Fleetwood Mac's 1975 self-titled album. More than twenty years later, Stevie rerecorded a 1998 solo version for the movie *Practical Magic.* Stevie actually wrote "Crystal" with her father and grandfather in mind, but that hasn't prevented couples from choosing it as their wedding song.

For someone who has repeatedly walked through the fire in many senses—in tumultuous relationships and tragic life events and music industry politics—Stevie has never come out on the other side bitter. Her romance is a renewable energy source, constantly inspiring new songs and younger artists, fans, and acolytes.

"To inspire people, to make people feel things—that's why we do this," Stevie has said of her never-ending drive to tap into the most primal emotion. "Maybe you want to make people sob the way we were sobbing the other night at the movies—me and two friends, all of us sobbing so hard we can't even look at each other—that's actually a really beautiful thing. If you can't do that or if you can't make somebody laugh and remember the first time they ever fell in love, then you should just stop."

Lest you walk away from this chapter thinking that Stevie doesn't temper her romanticism with a bit of practicality, here's a sensible piece of advice from her: "You should not destroy your former career by trying to keep things going if you don't have it anymore and the work isn't coming from the right place. You should just count your money and make investments in real estate and be done. That's it. You should just go to do something else."

LESSON TWELVE

DON'T BE AFRAID OF CHANGING

Everyone else changes. I don't change.

—Stevie Nicks, The Guardian, 1998

Change is like death. Both are inevitable, and we hate having to think about either. Well, maybe one more than the other—death kind of wins out against most things we dread. (I know for me, I can barely deal with sudden shifts in plans without spinning out.) But one of the best ways of coping with change is to look at it right in the face and acknowledge that no matter how hard we rail against it, change *will* happen. So why not try to befriend it? Or at the very least, acknowledge its inevitability? Maybe even, like Stevie, channel our feelings about change into something creative?

Today, Stevie might be our rock 'n' roll godmother—an eternal fairy princess from a higher dimension. But never forget that she is still a human being, and much of her knowledge has been earned through lived experience, which always includes change.

Despite her anxiety around leaving home and the familiarity of the Bay Area scene in her Fritz days, Stevie embraced the move to Los Angeles. Her motivation was not unique—the tenuous hope that the city of dreams would launch her to global recognition as a singer, songwriter, and band member.

By the late seventies, Stevie had more than achieved that goal. She was arguably the most recognizable member of

Fleetwood Mac, partially due to her witchy stage presence, but also because she appeared so prominently on the cover of *Rumours,* which became the band's first number one album on the UK Albums Chart, topped the U.S. *Billboard* 200, and won the Album of the Year Grammy in 1978. Their follow-up album, *Tusk,* was less well received, with critics calling it overly long and self-indulgent. Radio programmers opted out of playing it because they felt it didn't sound enough like Fleetwood Mac. But Stevie's contributions, including "Sara," the achingly ethereal "Storms," and the slow-building "Sisters of the Moon," made the two-album *Tusk* more accessible in the present-day pop space, while Lindsey, who'd completely embraced the burgeoning punk movement, veered off into a more distinctly experimental zone with offbeat rhythms and Talking Headsesque sing-speak refrains.

Tusk has long since been reevaluated in a much more positive light, and deservedly so. Christine McVie's contributions "Think About Me" and "Over and Over" touched the pop pulse with every bit as much precision as Stevie's compositions. If *Tusk* sounds disjointed, that's likely because its main writers were looking in different directions, each in their own world of creation, trying to fit their increasingly disparate voices onto one record. Fleetwood Mac was growing out of sync. Change was imminent.

Stevie had been considering a solo move for a little while. Paul Fishkin, who was president of Bearsville Records, initially saw the potential in Stevie's going solo when they briefly dated during the *Rumours* era. Meanwhile, Danny Goldberg had recently started working with Stevie on the PR side to help her branch out into fashion, film projects, and possibly a solo career, which still was entirely theoretical. Stevie was still feeling hurt over the fact that "Silver Springs" had been left off *Rumours;* meanwhile, she was experiencing a growing cognitive dissonance around the fact that her songs were seen as the centerpiece of every Fleetwood Mac album she'd been part of, but the machinery behind the band tended to dismiss her.

Despite the overwhelming success of her songs "Dreams" and "Rhiannon," Stevie actually wielded very little power in Fleetwood Mac. Prior to that, she'd wielded very little power in her dynamic with Lindsey, who she felt never took her seriously and was always tinkering too much with her songs. "Though he loved me . . . he was much enamored with taking my songs and changing them, which always hurt me," she said in 1988. "As much as I loved him, as much as I cared about him, it was very hard for me to walk away and leave him one of my songs because I never knew what he was going to do with it." Stevie needed to break off on her own on a soul level. This was the only way she'd truly grow as an artist and a person.

As Fleetwood Mac readied *Tusk* for release, Stevie, Paul, and Danny worked quietly on the side to build their own boutique label, Modern Records, which would incubate and distribute her future solo work. After Fleetwood Mac completed their Tusk tour in December 1979, Stevie signed a deal with Atlantic Records—something she could legally do because Warners never thought to include a solo clause in Fleetwood Mac's contract.

Once word got out to Mick Fleetwood and Warner Bros., Mick was enraged. Fleetwood Mac's lawyer tried to claim Stevie's solo venture was going to prevent the band from getting a better royalty deal on the renegotiated Warner contract Mick was working on. The band as a whole felt paranoid that Stevie, one of their biggest selling points, had designs to leave them altogether, which she promised she had no plans to do. Stevie's primary reason for going solo was rooted in artistic expression and the lack of opportunity for it in a personality-filled band like Fleetwood Mac. She had a backlog of songs she wanted the chance to record and release on her terms.

Despite having every practical reason to go solo, Stevie had no guarantee that her move would be a success. Today, we're used to pop stars starting out in bands and transitioning to solo careers: Beyoncé and Destiny's Child; Justin Timberlake in *NSYNC; Michael Jackson in the Jackson 5; Ricky Martin in Menudo; practically every member of Fifth Harmony and One Direction. But in the 1970s, going solo was seen as a riskier prospect. Solo albums by artists in big bands tended not to do big numbers (according to Danny Goldberg) unless they had hit singles bolstered by plenty of radio play. After *Tusk* failed to live up to the smash-hit *Rumours,* Fleetwood Mac's stock had taken a dip.

Stevie had no idea whether her venture would pay off without the safety net of Fleetwood Mac. Meanwhile, the industry acted unsure as to whether her fairy-gypsy shtick could successfully carry an entire album. But she was thinking long-term about her viability as an artist and felt going solo was the strategic right choice—even if her most die-hard fans mourned the rumors that Fleetwood Mac was over and felt Stevie's own career was now on the wane.

"I just decided when I came off the yearlong Tusk tour that I wasn't going to give up my life and die a lonely, overdone, overused rock star," Stevie told *BAM* magazine in 1981. "I didn't want to be written up in fifty years as a miserable old woman who never got to do anything but tour and be famous for ten years and then everything was over."

"'Bella donna' is a term of endearment I use," she told *Rolling Stone* in 1981 of the name for her debut solo album, "and the title is about making a lot of decisions in my life, making a change based on the turmoil in my soul. You get to a certain age where you want to slow down, be quieter. The title song was basically a warning to myself and a question to others. I'm thirty-three years old, and my life has been very up and down in the last six years."

(While this might be one version of the truth about *Bella Donna,* Stevie's studio debut was nearly called *Belladonna* after the poisonous nightshade plant. Stevie was eventually convinced to change it ever so slightly, as her team felt anxious that the former title wouldn't go over well in Ronald and Nancy Reagan's "Just Say No" America.)

Fortunately for all involved, Stevie's solo entry with *Bella Donna* was a resounding success. The album went number one (for one week, but still, a number one is a number one) and sold three million copies before the end of 1981. The newly launched MTV also gave it a boost by playing the Tom Petty and the Heartbreakers–accompanied lead single "Stop Draggin' My Heart Around" on repeat. The risk had paid off. Given how fractured Fleetwood Mac had become by 1980, and how badly each of its members needed a break from the others, a change was coming regardless of what the future held. Sure, there were some hurt egos all around—Lindsey infamously liked to name-call the Tom Petty duet "Stop Draggin' My Career Around" and allegedly barely acknowledged *Bella Donna* or its success. (His own solo venture, 1981's *Law and Order,* peaked at only number 32 on the *Billboard* chart.)

"I took Lindsey in a copy of the record right when it was fresh off the press, and I signed it and said a lot of really wonderful things to him," Stevie said in 1995. "I set it up on the console, and he moved it and put it down on the floor, just kind of leaning against one of the steps in the studio room. And I watched him all day long, from three in the afternoon until three or four the next morning, and he walked right out that room without the record. And I never forgave him for that."

While hurt and disappointed at her ex's behavior, Stevie was thrilled and gratified at what was happening with her solo career. Now she was *Rolling Stone*'s "Reigning Queen of Rock and Roll." With her potent mixture of premonition and clear-eyed ambition, she had faced down impending change and bent it to her will.

But not all change is good. It wasn't long after the release of *Bella Donna* and Fleetwood Mac's next album, *Mirage,* that Stevie lost her closest friend in the world, who was also like a family member to Fleetwood Mac, Robin Anderson, who died in October 1982. To say Stevie was inconsolable would be a massive understatement. And while some of her subsequent decisions were ill-advised (as she herself has admitted plenty of times), Stevie poured her grief into the *Mirage* single "Gypsy," a ruminating minor-key confessional dedicated to Robin, and into the subsequent creation of what would become her second solo album: *The Wild Heart.*

While *Bella Donna* had been decades in the making, *The Wild Heart* more closely reflected life events Stevie had endured in the previous couple of years. As she traveled with Kim Anderson to their honeymoon at San Ysidro Ranch near Santa Barbara, Stevie heard Prince's popular tune "Little Red Corvette" on the radio. Inspired by Prince's use of glowing synths and reverb-soaked drum machines, Stevie ended up writing and recording part of "Stand Back" that night.

The disco-leaning lead single of 1983's *The Wild Heart* marked a sonic shift for Stevie's solo work, which she introduced by sounding as close to Tom Petty and the Heartbreakers as possible without literally joining the Heartbreakers on *Bella Donna*. By comparison, *The Wild Heart* adopted a more of-the-moment soft pop / adult contemporary eighties aesthetic (though Stevie did bring Tom Petty and the Heartbreakers back for "I Will Run to You"—once a Heartbreaker, always a Heartbreaker). Prince himself visited Sunset Sound to play the synth on "Stand Back," though he refused to be credited. ("Prince leaves no clues. We have an understanding, we're friends, and whatever he wants is fine. I just wanted him to play," Stevie told MTV about this.) The credit ended up going to Sandy Stewart, a new creative collaborator who helped Stevie write through this period of her life, one marked by the loss of Robin and surging demand for a follow-up album to *Bella Donna*.

On the cover of *The Wild Heart,* three versions of Stevie appear. One is crouched low in grief. The middle image stands facing to the side in a dark, hooded robe, representing the reincarnated soul of Robin. The third is Stevie in full "Queen of Rock" form. She dedicated *The Wild Heart* to Robin, writing "And . . . 'Just like the white winged dove' / This music is dedicated to Robin—for her brave, wild heart / And to the gypsies—that remain."

The Wild Heart also represented another big step away from Fleetwood Mac, with Stevie feeling out the ways she'd changed and grown more into herself as a performer now firmly in her thirties. "With *The Wild Heart* . . . it's probably the one time in my life where I'm really going through the 'edge of seventeen,' the edge of getting enough older that I might not be as wild as I am now," she told MTV. "But now, it's a special time, 'cause I feel wild. And with my audiences . . . I feel we're all in love. I feel it when I walk onstage. To me, that's very real and very deep."

Stevie's greatest career asset has been in her ability to embrace change. Unlike some popular artists who grow visibly complacent in their star power, Stevie has found ways forward by facing down her greatest challenges. We'll get into some of her health challenges in the next chapter, but let's take a moment to study a long-standing interpersonal obstacle going by the name of Lindsey Buckingham.

Lindsey had been a problem area for Stevie in innumerable ways that went well beyond their romantic dissolution in the seventies. They found a way to work together in Fleetwood Mac; their collective ambition overcame any hurt feelings (and there were plenty of those). But Lindsey was flat-out unsupportive of Stevie's solo work, which he barely acknowledged. Even worse, Stephen Davis's *Gold Dust Woman* alleged that Lindsey physically abused Stevie multiple times over their forty-year association. Sometimes, the physical abuse would leak out into the public eye. In an infamous 1980 Tusk concert in Wellington, New Zealand, Lindsey came at Stevie multiple times onstage while she was singing "Rhiannon." At a previous show on that tour in Australia, he'd rudely mocked her dramatic, drapey performance style by pulling his jacket up over his head, imitating her shawl. This time around, he tried to kick her. He hurled his black Les Paul guitar at her. If Stevie hadn't instinctively ducked, she could have been hospitalized, or worse. "He was mad at me probably because he . . . It was okay for me to be the performer that I was when we were a couple, but when we broke up, he hated that fact that I was such a lead singer," Stevie later recalled. "And I'm sure when we left New Zealand, we were not even on the same plane." (When asked about that incident, Lindsey admitted that it sounded like something he'd do but claimed not to remember details.)

Only Christine McVie stood up in Stevie's defense after the New Zealand show. Marching up to Lindsey, Christine slapped him across the face. "I think he's the only person I ever, ever slapped," Christine later told *Rolling Stone*. "I actually might have chucked a glass of wine, too. I just didn't think it was the way to treat a paying audience. I mean, aside from making a mockery of Stevie like that. Really unprofessional, over the top. Yes, she cried. She cried a lot."

The Les Paul / kicking incident, unfortunately, would not be the last time Lindsey got physical with Stevie. In 1987, during a heated argument with the rest of the band, Lindsey slapped Stevie, pushed her up against a car hood, and put his hands around her neck. "I thought he was going to kill me," Stevie said.

Today, as I am writing this, Lindsey and Stevie have fallen out for good, the band having kicked the guitarist out in 2018 and hiring Mike Campbell of Tom Petty and the Heartbreakers and Neil Finn of Crowded House in his place.

In 2013, Mick asked Stevie if she would consider touring with Fleetwood Mac again—with Lindsey in tow. She agreed—on the condition that Lindsey behave himself around her. Nearly half a century after the two musicians had first met as teenagers, their dynamic hardly resembled what it once had. In the beginning, Stevie was largely dependent on Lindsey for industry contacts, song arrangement ideas, and general opportunities. Their destinies were bound up together in the foundational days of Fritz and Buckingham Nicks. Now, however, the tables had turned. Stevie was an international music icon—the Queen of Rock and Roll. Lindsey was well respected and had a thriving core fan base, but his name didn't spark the same recognition on a global scale. If Fleetwood Mac was going to reunite, it had better be a positive experience for all involved. For a while, it was.

Until 2018. "It happened one night, not planned, at a MusiCares [benefit concert]," Stevie told *Rolling Stone*. "I didn't even tell anybody it had happened until the whole ceremony was over. I took with me that night a song that I had done with LeAnn Rimes called 'Borrowed.' I took it with me to play for him because I thought we could do this song beautifully.

"That's when he wasn't very nice to anybody; he wasn't very nice to Harry Styles. I could hear my mom saying, 'Are you really going to spend the next fifteen years of your life with this man?' I could hear my very pragmatic father—and, by the way, my mom and dad liked Lindsey a lot—saying, 'It's time for you guys to get a divorce.' Between those two, I said, 'I'm done.'

"I dealt with Lindsey for as long as I could," Stevie concluded. "You could not say that I did not give him more than three hundred million chances."

Even if mixed with relief, it must have been tremendously painful for Stevie to finally say "No more" to Lindsey, with whom she'd built a successful—if endlessly fraught—music empire, one beloved by generations of fans, many of whom still hold out hope for an onstage reunion.

They might just get their wish. In July 2025, passersby noticed a mysterious billboard hoisted above Sunset Boulevard in Los Angeles. Located not very far from Sound City Studios, where Stevie and Lindsey once spent hours recording in their pre–Fleetwood Mac days, the billboard displayed the artwork for *Buckingham Nicks* alongside a forthcoming date: September 19. Meanwhile, both Stevie and Lindsey were sharing coordinated lyrics from their song "Frozen Love" on social media. Fans speculated that the duo's long out-of-print *Buckingham Nicks* album from 1973 would be getting a proper reissue, and they were right. Could this mean that the long-mythologized couple were getting back on decent terms?

Yes, no, and maybe. Despite such a major milestone (*Buckingham Nicks* had not been reissued in fifty years), which kicked off a flurry of media speculation around a possible reunion between the former bandmates/lovers, the *Buckingham Nicks* reissue appeared to be just that—a reissue and not much else. Aside from a "happy birthday" wish from Stevie's Instagram to Lindsey's, there was no accompanying Buckingham Nicks reunion tour, no promotional events, no reason for Stevie and Lindsey to be in the same room at the same time.

But Fleetwood Mac's tectonic plates are constantly shifting. When I turned in the first draft of this book, Stevie and Lindsey had not yet announced their reissue. When I sat down to go over its edits, as of October 2025, new reports were surfacing that Mick Fleetwood was "leading peace talks" between the estranged duo as the band mapped out plans to celebrate fifty years of *Rumours.* Allegedly Stevie and Lindsey were now on "a healing journey" toward reconciliation, yet again. By the time this book goes to print, who knows where the winds of change will have taken them?

Change has a way of happening no matter what we do. The only way out is through. As Stevie once put it: "I've learned as time passes, all the things you're afraid of will come and they will go, and you'll be all right."

LESSON THIRTEEN

ONLY YOU CAN SAVE YOURSELF

Writers do not thrive on drugs like Klonopin and Prozac. It takes your soul; it takes your creativity; it takes your love of running home at night and getting out a typewriter or getting out your paper and pencil and writing something that you love. It takes that away. You don't care anymore... And that's horrible to me. One of the few things that I've never not done in my life is not care. And I didn't care for a long time.

—Stevie Nicks, CDNow, 2001

The hedonism of the 1960s and '70s can't be overstated. Drugs. Sex. Drugs before sex. Sex while doing drugs. As a child of the D.A.R.E. generation, I can't pretend to know much about it beyond what I've seen in movies and read in archived interviews. My primary takeaway about the mind-bent sixties and seventies is that substances were so ubiquitous and free-flowing that they were just *normal*.

For Stevie Nicks, who came of age in the sixties and shot to rock stardom in the seventies—decades defined by endless partying with fountains of alcohol, strips of LSD, loopifying Quaaludes, magic mushrooms, and lines of cocaine, among other intoxicants—the singer fell right into the scene. She barely made it out alive.

Famously, Stevie's substance of choice was cocaine, which flowed backstage along with champagne. Coke had an emboldening effect on Stevie, who appreciated the boost in courage as she stepped onstage to perform, participated in interviews, went in for costume fittings, and sought distraction from the growing isolation that comes with global fame—all the pressures that came along with her newfound rock star status. "I used to carry a gram of cocaine in my boot at all times," she later told *Oprah's Master Class*. "And it was the first thing I thought of when I woke up in the morning and the last thing I thought of before I went to bed." And speaking of going to bed, Stevie's purse was also allegedly full of tranquilizing pills like Quaaludes to help her catch a few hours' sleep before the circus started again.

Though Stevie didn't indulge much prior to joining Fleetwood Mac, her recreational usage started increasing after she teamed up with the group. But her overreliance kicked into high gear as Fleetwood Mac's *Rumours* took off. At one point, she was spending millions on the white powder, which was burning a literal hole in her nose. "All of us were drug addicts . . . but there was a point where I was the worst drug addict," Stevie told *Rolling Stone* in 2015. "I was a girl, I was fragile, and I was doing a lot of coke. And I had that hole in my nose. So it was dangerous."

Though her substance use wouldn't reach the breaking point until the mideighties, Stevie experienced a flood of health issues and near misses well beforehand. Her consistent cocaine usage was influencing her already husky voice, deepening it to the point where one *Rolling Stone* critic likened it to Linda Blair's demon-possessed snarl in *The Exorcist*.

On the evening prior to the Rumours world tour, Fleetwood Mac received news that their album had just gone platinum. They were so elated that they took off partying in a blowout celebration that lasted almost two days. Stevie got so caught up in the madness that she forgot to take out her contact lenses, which damaged her corneas, nearly blinding her. The band's tour manager, John Courage, had to carry her out onto the stage on his back. She also had to avoid looking at the stage lights during performances. Soon, a doctor told her to bandage her eyes to let them heal so she wouldn't go blind.

Stevie has always claimed to have poor eyesight, but the contacts incident arguably made a bad situation worse. "I got diagnosed with this thing a year and a half ago called wet macular degeneration, and it is not a good thing," Stevie told *Rolling Stone* in 2024. (It should be said that AMD is a common age-related condition and is the leading cause of vision loss among people age fifty and older. Correlation doesn't equal causation, but Stevie's lifetime of eye issues probably didn't help.) "I was seeing all these colors, big things of purple. I was having, like, acid trips. And I'm going, 'I'm not taking any acid, so I don't understand what this is.' Now, every six, seven, eight, nine weeks, I have to have a shot in each one of my eyes. That's going to be for the rest of my life."

Stevie's drug use also had a crippling effect on her romantic relationships, though she wasn't at all alone there. She and Mick fell into each other's arms through a mutual haze of alcohol and cocaine, and Stevie's earth-moving romance with Joe Walsh was famously unstable owing to the collective amount of substances both took in.

As the mideighties set in and Stevie readied her next solo album, *Rock a Little,* the singer was visibly unwell. Keith Olsen, one of the album's producers, grew upset with Stevie because she was too high to sing in tune. After recording "Has Anyone Ever Written Anything for You," he stormed out of the studio and quit on the spot. Jimmy Iovine, Stevie's *Bella Donna* and *The Wild Heart* producer (and a romantic partner), also walked out. Stevie also struggled to film the videos for the singles "Talk to Me" and "I Can't Wait," which had her climbing and descending a staircase, which she almost fell down.

Speaking of that experience, Stevie later said that while she loved "I Can't Wait" and its accompanying video, "I look at my eyes, and I say to myself, 'Could you have laid off the pot, the coke, and the tequila for three days so you could have looked a little better? Because your eyes look like they're swimming.' It just makes me want to go back into that video and stab myself."

On the Rock a Little tour in 1986, Stevie's condition appeared more troubling than ever. Her performances were hit-or-miss; worst case, she'd be slurring her words and literally falling offstage. Her nose bled often. Rumors abounded about the hole in her nose, how she'd been inserting cocaine vaginally and anally.

When the tour reached Red Rocks Amphitheater near Denver, Colorado, Mick was there to join Stevie on percussion. But her haggard appearance frightened him so much that he took her aside for a heart-to-heart. "I don't want to be like this," Mick recalled Stevie saying when he spoke to the author Stephen Davis during the writing of *Gold Dust Woman*. "I don't want to need this stuff so much. I'm going to do something about it."

When the Rock a Little tour concluded and Stevie was back in Los Angeles, her team staged an intervention. It wasn't just the cocaine that had become a major problem—Stevie had been relying more and more on alcohol and various other methods of self-medication, including snorting aspirin dissolved in water to help with her migraines. "I thought I was being the best, most hygienic nurse ever," she told *Rolling Stone* in 2015. A doctor told her that the hole in her nasal cavity could cause a brain hemorrhage the next time she used. The longer Stevie went without getting help, the likelier it was that she'd die. Friends even began to anticipate getting the dreaded phone call. "I did all I could to talk her into getting some help and getting right," Tom Petty told *Rolling Stone*. "I was very worried about her. To the point that if the phone did ring and they said, 'Stevie died,' I wouldn't have been surprised."

Around this time, Stevie wrote "Mabel Normand," which chronicled her addiction and later found its release on 2014's *24 Karat Gold: Songs from the Vault*. Named for the Hollywood actress who died of tuberculosis in 1930 after many years of cocaine and alcohol addiction, "Mabel Normand" was Stevie's reflection on her own disease—and how close she came to death. "In 1985, I was dancing at the edge of danger myself, just like she was," Stevie told *Out* magazine. "I was just doing so much coke. And it had already backfired on me completely. I saw this documentary, and I felt this union with her: Oh my God, the same thing that happened to this woman in the twenties is happening to me in the eighties—how can this be? Then she died, and that really scared me. She was rich, she was famous, she had everything. She had it all. And I very well could have died just as easily as she did. . . . That's when I wrote the song. Less than a year later, I went to rehab at Betty Ford."

"Mabel Normand" was not just a warning from Stevie to herself—she hoped it would speak to anyone else struggling through addiction. "I wanted it to be something that somebody having a problem with drugs can sit down and listen to five thousand times," she continued in 2014. "Try and let it be an epiphany for you, eighteen-year-old person that is doing a lot of coke and smoking heroin and taking ecstasy and is on a dead-end road to hell. I want them to hear the word 'cocaine' and think brain hemorrhage, beauty gone, lines, aging, fat."

Stevie described her decade of alcohol and drug use as a "wicked little circle . . . a rat's wheel" of "brandy, cigarettes, pot, and coke. You'd do some coke and you were nervous, you'd smoke some pot to calm down, you were too stoned, and you'd do some more coke to wake up, and you'd have a drink because you were too nervous . . . it was just a nightmare."

When Stevie checked into the Betty Ford Center in Rancho Mirage, California, she used the name Sara Anderson. The facility was no vacation, either. Part of treatment included manual labor, like mopping floors and cleaning bathrooms (something Stevie had once done plenty of in her pre–Fleetwood Mac days). Later, she likened the experience to "the army. Betty's army. This is not celebrity rehab. This is hardcore rehab. There's nothing fun about it. It's not a spa."

Stevie chronicled her experiences in rehab on "Welcome to the Room . . . Sara," which appeared on Fleetwood Mac's 1987 album *Tango in the Night*. She wasn't as forthcoming with the press about the percussive song's meaning, preferring to talk around the subject rather than directly address it. " 'Welcome to the Room . . . Sara' is very much a secret kind of song," she told *Creem* magazine. "Sara is from *Tusk,* that's the same Sara we're talking about—and she just has some experiences that she's talking about. I don't really want anyone to know whether I'm going into her room or she's coming into mine, or what's in the room. This room is an ominous room. I'm not Bob Dylan, but every once in a while, I've gotta say something." (Mick Fleetwood revealed what "Welcome to the Room" was really about in his 1990 memoir, *Fleetwood: My Life and Adventures in Fleetwood Mac.*)

While Stevie emerged from the Betty Ford clinic cocaine-free, and managed to stay off the powder, she had a lot of work to do in terms of regaining the industry's full trust. At one time she had been perceived as the main attraction of Fleetwood Mac, but by the late eighties Stevie's team were all but certain she would succumb to her addictions. Even post-rehab, they weren't confident she'd stay clean—especially if she went on tour with Fleetwood Mac to promote *Tango in the Night*.

But Stevie wanted to keep working, and she had no interest in going to Alcoholics Anonymous, "because I wasn't an alcoholic." To accommodate her, Stevie's team of doctors, management, and advisers recommended that she start seeing a therapist, which she did. Stevie began seeing a well-known psychiatrist in Beverly Hills who suggested she minimize the possibility of a cocaine relapse by taking benzodiazepines—first Valium, then Xanax, and finally Klonopin.

At first, she appeared happy and lighter on her feet, even though many in her orbit thought she also seemed in a bit of a haze. When Stevie released her fourth solo album, 1989's *The Other Side of the Mirror,* she claimed it was "probably my favorite album. . . . I had gotten away from the cocaine. I spent a year writing those songs. I was drug-free, and I was happy."

It would take eight years before Stevie would realize what Klonopin had taken from her: creativity, verve, ambition, focus. When she told her psychiatrist about the anxiety she felt about writing new material for *The Other Side of the Mirror,* the doctor simply increased her dosage.

"It's a very subtle drug; you just don't feel it much, or so you think. On the bottle, it says: 'Take as needed.' That's the stupidest thing I've ever heard. So you think: 'Well, I need it every two hours.' It's addiction in a bottle," she told *The Guardian.* "It was a totally non-time. I just existed. It took away all my wonderful drama, my tempestuousness, my compassion, my empathy—all those things that drove me to my piano. I say to myself now: 'How did you survive eight years without your wonderful drama?'"

Stevie faced wave after wave of criticism in the late eighties, which no doubt fueled her growing Klonopin dependency. Reviewers had brutal things to say about her live shows; they chastised her weight gain, her corseted stage apparel, her too-big hair, her caked-on makeup. Reporters shouted rude and invasive questions about her time in rehab. Visibly exhausted, she'd recently been diagnosed with the Epstein-Barr virus. Fans and the industry at large seemed to doubt her viability as a performer and were starting to regard her as a washed-up has-been. All because she had the audacity to be a female pop singer over forty.

Also, Fleetwood Mac was falling apart again. Lindsey had left under extremely unpleasant circumstances in the summer of 1987 when he refused to tour *Tango in the Night.* When confronted by the rest of the band (including Stevie, who pleaded with him to reconsider), Lindsey grew irate and allegedly slapped his onetime musical partner across the face and tried to strangle her. "He's a thing of my past," she later told the BBC. "I hope he finds what he's searching for, and I hope he's happy, and I wish him well. And there's nothing left to say." Stevie left the band a few years later and returned only once, in 1993, to perform "Don't Stop" with the band at Bill Clinton's presidential inauguration.

As Stevie prepped her fifth album, *Street Angel,* her issues with Klonopin worsened. She felt it was making her look older than she was, she was always cold, and she'd developed tremors in her hands. "I was shaking so hard that people would look at me like I had Parkinson's disease. And then I'm starting to think, do I have some kind of neurological disease, and I'm dying?" Stevie asked her doctor, what if we decreased my dosage? But he replied that decreasing her Klonopin dosage would only make her "nervous." Plus, lots of famous singers take it: Aerosmith's Steven Tyler, Prince, others. You're in good company, Stevie. What if instead I *increase* your dose?

Stevie was at a loss. She never realized the addictive nature of benzodiazepines; she'd simply been taking the drug as prescribed. "Like Vitamin C," she told VH1.

"This doctor was a groupie—he just wanted to hear me tell stories about rock and roll," Stevie also told *Rolling Stone.* "So he kept upping my dose for years. Finally, I said, 'I'm taking enough Klonopin every day to sink a boat. That's why

I gained all this weight, and that's why my writing is terrible, and that's why *The Other Side of the Mirror* was the last good record I made. This was all your idea.'"

The real tipping point came near the end of 1993. Stevie was hosting a baby shower at home and standing near the fireplace hearth. She blacked out and woke up "curled up by the fireplace. . . . I'd hit my head but felt no pain." Her guests quickly got Stevie into bed. Later, she got out and had a look in the mirror. "I had some blood on the side of my head. I never injure myself, so I was horrified to see that blood. I hadn't had enough wine to pass out like that. I knew it was the Klonopin."

Stevie had an idea. As an experiment, she asked her long-time friend Glenn Parish if he wouldn't mind taking her current prescribed dose of Klonopin to see how it affected him. (Keep in mind, it wasn't common knowledge yet that benzodiazepines were extremely addictive. It wasn't until 1990 that the American Psychiatric Association launched a task force to investigate the dangers of rising benzodiazepine prescriptions. Despite its findings that up to 80 percent of those taking these drugs would experience withdrawal upon cessation, that did little to reduce the skyrocketing number of prescriptions in the 1990s.)

Glenn started to set up a stereo but had to stop midway. "He was almost hallucinating. It was bad. Then he just passed out." Stevie called her psychiatrist in a panic. "'I gave Glenn everything you prescribed for me.' And the first words out of his mouth were, 'Are you trying to kill him?' And the next words out of my mouth were, 'Are you trying to kill *me*?'"

Stevie checked into Daniel Freeman Memorial Hospital in Venice Beach and remained there for the next forty-seven days. Purging her system of benzodiazepines was a far more painful process than coming off cocaine ever was. Describing the debilitating detox process, she said, "It took forty-seven days for me to detox from Klonopin. It was horrible. My hair turned gray. My skin molted. I couldn't sleep. I was in so much pain. Legs aching. Body cramps. The rock star in me wanted to get in a limousine and go to Cedars Sinai and say, 'Give me some Demerol, because I am in pain.' And the other side of me said, 'You will fight out these forty-seven days.'"

Stevie fought. And when those forty-seven days were up, she emerged from the hospital with "a new lease on life." She elaborated: "I learned so much in that hospital. I wrote the whole time I was in there, some of my best writing ever. I learned that I could have fun and laugh and cry with amazing people and not be on drugs. I learned that I could live my life and still be beautiful and have fun and go to parties and not even have a glass of wine. And I never went to therapy again." I mean, would *you* go back to therapy if you'd been overprescribed an addictive, potentially life-ending pharmaceutical?

Few people in her life would likely describe Stevie as

I learned that I could have fun and laugh and cry with amazing people and not be on drugs. I learned that I could live my life and still be beautiful and have fun and go to parties and not even have a glass of wine.

angry or a grudge holder. But she reserved whatever anger she was capable of for that psychiatrist, whom she (understandably) has in recent years referred to as "Doctor Fuckhead."

The source of Stevie's anger lay in the drug's having sapped her ability to live and work with the zeal and ambition that had defined her life and career up until then. Klonopin's tranquilizing properties took away her inherent ability to think, move, and create—everything that had ever been important to Stevie. She told *60 Minutes Australia* in 2017: "In that eight years [on Klonopin], I could have had a baby. I could have had maybe an amazing relationship. I might have been married. I could have done another two Fleetwood Mac albums that were really great. Maybe I could have done another two or three Stevie Nicks albums. . . . So many things that I could have accomplished during that eight long years. I accomplished nothing. That's my regret. If I were to see that psychiatrist on the street, I would run towards him and kill him."

In the years after her second time in rehab, Stevie spoke passionately about the dangers of Klonopin addiction and everything she learned in her struggle to get clean. Immediately after rehab, and after releasing *Street Angel,* she spoke apologetically about her fifth album's low energy. "I'd been taking Klonopin for almost eight years," she told *Time Out*. "*Street Angel* was done in the last two years of that, when it had kicked in to the point that it took away my soul and my creativity, . . . I listened to the record—I'm off all the drugs—and I knew it was terrible. It had cost a fortune."

In later interviews, Stevie displayed the immense insight she'd gained about why she'd leaned so hard into substances—beyond the fact that she was a rock star, and they were endlessly available and unregulated. "The truth about drugs is how they are usually a symptom of an even bigger problem—in my case, an ego out of control," she said.

> Sometimes the biggest and most dangerous lies are the ones we tell ourselves. With fame comes the danger of thinking that you are bigger and better than anyone else, and that you can live "above it all." Letting your ego get out of control can often bring you crashing back down to earth. Like a drug, your ego can stop you from listening to your true self. . . . My true self is someone who writes and sings songs. Then I get to perform those songs—bringing them alive for other people! It's such an honor to be able to do that: to go around the world and see how your songs—your children in a way—are so deeply loved, understood, and appreciated by others who only know you through your words and music. Sometimes it feels like a lot of work, but ultimately it's a privilege. Too many of us who have succeeded in the popular arts have somehow forgotten that.

> My best advice goes well beyond just staying away from drugs. Check your ego, too! If you're lucky enough to figure out what you are meant to do with your life, follow that passion. For me it was music, but I had to act on that passion to make my dreams come true.

Stevie never relapsed into either substance. She still smokes "a little bit of pot," telling *Rolling Stone:* "It's my one little thing that I can do. If I'm sitting at the piano and I'm writing, then I'm not out driving around in a car. Nobody is here, nobody sees me. I am not smoking with anybody. It's just me, and it's my choice. I use it as a tool, and I'm very careful, you know? And I get results. However, if I thought it was going to lead me back to something worse, I'd stop."

LESSON FOURTEEN

DON'T LET THEM TAKE YOUR POWER

Now more than ever, it's important for us to continue to fight for what we believe in. And for me, I will not stop fighting for reproductive freedom.

—Stevie Nicks, Instagram, 2024

Stevie Nicks did not start out political. Despite coming of age in the protest-heavy Bay Area in the 1960s, politics and protest were not part of her musicianship—in Fleetwood Mac or otherwise. Mick Fleetwood used to like to say that the band lived in "the Bubble," meaning that they were more or less ignorant to whatever went on outside themselves and their entourage. In the 1970s, Stevie made a point to stay out of politics, and even once admonished Jackson Browne for getting arrested at an antinuclear demonstration at the Diablo Canyon reactor in Northern California. "I'm not a martyr," she told him when he suggested Fleetwood Mac get involved with the antinuclear movement. "I would much rather be around to write the story than die for it and leave nothing behind. I believe you should put your talent where your talent is and stay out of the rest of it.

"We're not a political group," she added. "My mission is not to stand on a political soapbox." In other instances, the ultragirly Stevie shied away from the "women's liberation" title, believing feminists of the day to be aggressive on the whole—a far cry from her personality. (Later, Stevie would confirm that she does identify as a feminist.)

Much later, as the 2020 U.S. presidential election loomed, Stevie revealed that she didn't even vote until she was seventy.

"But now I regret that," she admitted. "And I've told everybody that onstage for the last two years. I regret that, and I don't have very many regrets."

If you place yourself in Stevie's platform boots, it's easy to see why she would shift to a more vocal political platform, even within the last decade. For starters, the twenty-four-hour news cycle—launched in 1980 with CNN and evolved with the internet, social media, and mobile push notifications—has made it next to impossible to disengage from current events. Simply put, the way Western society consumes the news has evolved to such a degree that detaching from it is next to impossible, and it's become far more commonplace for high-profile entertainers to endorse political candidates, attend campaign events, or make public statements about causes during live shows. In Stevie's earliest years, singers like Bob Dylan, Joan Baez, and Pete Seeger regularly raised their voices to condemn societal and political ills. But popular artists could also just as easily encase themselves in a "bubble" of nonstop touring life, substances, love affairs, recording sessions, and parties. Politics need not apply.

But Fleetwood Mac and Stevie Nicks never existed in a vacuum. Both entities have shifted their stances in various ways. For Fleetwood Mac, the band made American and music history by reuniting to perform the campaign theme song "Don't Stop (Thinking About Tomorrow)" at Bill Clinton's 1993 inaugural ball when he won the presidency. Stevie was so adamant that every (disbanded) member show up for this honor that she personally called Lindsey (who, let's not forget, had tried to strangle her only a few years prior) to demand that he show up. "If you cheat me out of this honoring moment, I'll never speak to you again," she told him, a moment Zoë Howe chronicles in her 2015 rock biography *Stevie Nicks: Visions, Dreams, and Rumours.*

Just being part of the Clinton inauguration events was a tremendously gratifying experience for Stevie and Fleetwood Mac, who at one point in their performance invited the sax-playing president onstage with them. "The [inaugural gala] was something I don't think any of us will ever forget," Stevie told the *Miami Herald*. "Walking out [onstage] and knowing we were walking out because Bill Clinton wanted us. You couldn't feel more special than we did that night."

In the early nineties, it was en vogue to be a celebrity aligning yourself with Clinton, who was largely regarded as the young, hip alternative to the stodgy, conservative Bush administration. When Clinton famously broke out his saxophone on *The Arsenio Hall Show,* he instantly endeared himself to younger voters and the celebrity class, Stevie among them.

Stevie took another step toward using her platform for positive change in 2005. This was post-9/11, and the United States was newly at war with Iraq and Afghanistan. In the early days of the conflict, patriotism was still all the rage. As she and Don Henley teamed up for their Two Voices tour, Stevie received a request to visit the Walter Reed Army Hospital in Washington, D.C., to spend some time with wounded soldiers. The experience had a profound effect on Stevie, who later wrote in her journal, "I look at life through the eyes of a rock and roll fairy princess who lives for nothing more than to sing a song . . . break a few hearts . . . and fly on to the next city . . . until today.

"I walked into Walter Reed today as a single woman with no children. I walked out a mother, a wife, a girlfriend, a sister, a daughter, a nurse, a patient's advocate—a changed woman. What I saw today will never leave my heart." Stevie also gave the soldiers iPods that came preloaded with a playlist of her favorite songs in the hope that the music would help them through their worst times, as it had done for her. Supplying iPods to soldiers would also become part of what Stevie did with her Soldier's Angel Foundation, which she founded in 2006.

In 2011, Stevie channeled her feelings into music on the sobering "Soldier's Angel," which appeared on *In Your Dreams*. It echoed her 1991 *Timespace* song "Desert Angel," which drew a connection between the American soldiers fighting the Gulf War and her native state of Arizona. ("I was still trying to figure out what I could write [in a letter] to the ones in the Gulf who are alone and scared . . . and I also knew I would write a song called 'Desert Angel' . . . and I would send them my feeling of sanctuary," she wrote in the *Timespace* liner notes.)

"This song is from a poem written after my second visit to

Walter Reed and Bethesda hospitals," she said about "Soldier's Angel."

> I printed the poem, all verses of it, and started to give it out to the soldiers and their families every time I visited. I always told them that someday it would be a song. But I could never write a chorus—those few lines eluded me. When I was in London with Fleetwood Mac in November 2009, an extremely tragic incident in Iraq concerning seven English soldiers caused a four-page journal entry where I pulled the four-line chorus. I asked Lindsey to help me record it—which brought Buckingham/Nicks back to life on this, my most revered song.
>
> My experience spending time with our wounded warriors at Walter Reed Hospital over the years has taught me more about heroism and humanity than I can ever possibly say here. The honor has been all mine, and this song is for all of them and their families.

Even when she wasn't overtly political, Stevie could never ignore instances of human suffering, whether it related to war or natural disasters. Her music took a humanitarian turn in 2011's "New Orleans," a song that mourned the losses and destruction of Hurricane Katrina, which hit New Orleans and its surrounding areas in 2005. "My mind immediately went to the fact that for a long time, my father was president of Greyhound," Stevie said in her 2013 *In Your Dreams* documentary about watching the news of the hurricane and its tragic aftermath, which was worsened by a severe lack of federal government aid. "I thought, if my dad was still alive, he would have had every Greyhound bus in this country on its way to get these people. And where in the heck is everybody? . . . That the United States of America would let those people sit there, where dogs were attacking people and kids were being raped in the dark. Your worst nightmare.

"I was horrified. I immediately started writing my poem. I had to be very careful as a songwriter. I was conflicted on how much I could say. Yes, you have to say, 'We may never forgive you, government of the United States, for not coming to our aid. But we are a flamboyant city, and we are a city of music, so we will come back.'"

Later, as discussed in the chapter on belief in crystal visions, Stevie released her first overt protest song, "Show Them the Way," in 2020, when the world was still reeling from the COVID-19 pandemic. It had been inspired by a dream she had in 2008 in which John F. Kennedy and Dr. Martin Luther King, Jr., appeared. "I hope that this song and its words will be seen as a prayer—a prayer for our country—a prayer for our world," she wrote in a press release for her first new song in six years. She also dedicated the track's piano version to the then presidential candidate and his running mate, Joe Biden and Kamala Harris.

As the growing political divide became harder to ignore, especially in the post-pandemic years, Stevie grew much more vocal and specific in her advocacy. In 2024, Stevie released the protest anthem "The Lighthouse"—a feminist call to arms sparked by the overturning of *Roe v. Wade*. With her good friend and fellow musician Sheryl Crow on guitar, Stevie compared herself to a lighthouse—a beacon guiding women to stand up to anyone who would erase their bodily autonomy.

"When *Roe v. Wade* was banished, I turned on *Morning Joe* and I swear to God, I thought Mika [Brzezinski] was going to crawl over the desk," Stevie told *Rolling Stone*.

> What she did was remind me what a loss this was. Because I can remember being so happy when it came into being in 1973. It was like we were safe.
>
> It's not just about not being careful and having an abortion. It's everything. It's all the health care. It's an ec-

topic pregnancy. It's all the procedures that need to be done in our bodies that half of us don't ever have and half of us have a whole lot more than other people. I was just really freaked out after I saw [the news], and that was the inspiration for this song.

I wrote the words in the morning. I never write in the morning, and I hadn't even had a cup of coffee. But I just wrote the whole thing. Then I closed the book and went back to sleep. It sounds like Marvin Gaye walking down a seedy alley and singing about life, and he runs into Dave Grohl and the Foo Fighters when he turns the corner. That's how I hear it.

Stevie was thinking about her own experience with abortion, too—the one she'd undergone only a few years after the procedure was legalized in the United States. The one that allowed her to continue in Fleetwood Mac and fully realize her dreams. "[Fleetwood Mac would have been] done. And that would've been sad, because I would not have married Don Henley," Stevie said. "That was a really fun relationship, but he was in a bigger band than me. Those boys were rock stars, par extraordinaire. Nobody in that band was ready to get married and have children. So I knew it would just be on me, and I wouldn't have even known what to do with that responsibility.

"I have a friend who had an ectopic pregnancy," she con-

We said we will never ever be treated like a second-class citizen amongst our peers as we get more famous and more famous—and if we're in a room with famous rock 'n' roll stars that are men and they treat us that way, we will scream at them and then we'll walk out.

tinued. "She went on to have a little girl who is my little soulmate goddaughter that I absolutely adore. She would've died if this had been the old days. And this little girl that I love so much would not be on this earth."

This sentiment echoed some anxiety Stevie had voiced earlier. "We fought very hard for feminism, for women's rights," Nicks told a crowd at South by Southwest in 2013. "What I'm seeing today is a very opposite thing. I don't know why, but I see women being put back in their place. And I hate it. We're losing all we worked so hard for, and it really bums me out."

When Stevie spoke out about her choice to have an abortion, she was well aware of the potential for pushback. She met that very real possibility with a shrug. "If people want to be mad at me, be mad at me," Stevie told CBS. "I don't care. Had I made the other choice, had I gone the other way, I'd have been a great mom. I went this way, and I've done great."

Even if she didn't realize it at the time, Stevie had represented a lighthouse in the popular music industry since the beginning of her career. Her very existence as a sexually liberated young woman fronting a popular rock band of mostly men moved the cultural needle when she joined Fleetwood Mac.

By demanding that she and Christine McVie be paid the same as every other member of Fleetwood Mac, and by teaming up with her bandmate to demand respect, and by being unafraid to express her femininity onstage, Stevie communicated to the world how she wanted to be seen and treated in a time when women were fighting for social equality on nearly every level of existence. "I think I've been very lucky," she said. "And maybe it's because when I joined Fleetwood Mac, Christine and I made a pact. We said we will never ever be treated like a second-class citizen amongst our peers as we get more famous and more famous—and if we're in a room with famous rock 'n' roll stars that are men and they treat us that way, we will scream at them and then we'll walk out.

"We've been a force of nature our entire career, so nobody has dared to step over that line to Christine McVie and Stevie Nicks," she continued. "I'm such a raging monster when I'm angry that it would have never worked, so I'm really glad I never had to run into that."

LESSON FIFTEEN

DON'T HAVE RIVALS. HAVE FRIENDS

Together, we are a serious force of nature, and it will give us the strength to maneuver the waters that are ahead of us.

—Stevie Nicks, The New Yorker, 2022

When we talk about Stevie Nicks's life and music, the singer's many romantic relationships tend to get top billing. But Stevie's friendships were every bit as foundational, if not more. For every infamous clash fans have read about between Stevie and Lindsey—and Stevie and Mick over "Silver Springs"—I bet you've almost never read about fraught internal band dynamics between Stevie and Christine McVie, Fleetwood Mac's only other female member. Because there weren't any.

In a society in which women are almost always pitted against one another, even when there's nothing actually wrong in their relationship, it was (and remains) remarkable that Stevie and Christine genuinely loved each other through everything. Even when they lost touch for a while in the eighties when the members of Fleetwood Mac were off doing solo projects, they could always come back together as if no time had passed.

While Lindsey sulked over Stevie's popularity in Fleetwood Mac and her subsequent solo success, Christine remained a source of support. (Not that she had much to complain about—Christine's contributions to the Fleetwood Mac catalog are every bit as substantial as Stevie's. If not for Christine McVie, we wouldn't have still ubiquitous pop gems like "Everywhere," "Little Lies," "Don't Stop," "Songbird," and "Say You Love Me," among others.)

"To be in a band with another girl who was this amazing musician—[Christine] kind of instantly became my best friend," Stevie told *The New Yorker* in 2022. "Christine was a whole other ballgame. She liked hanging out with the guys. She was just more comfortable with men than I had ever been."

When Mick first pushed to recruit Lindsey and Stevie into Fleetwood Mac, he asked Christine to sign off on the decision, as the drummer didn't want there to be a rivalry. "We met and I instantly liked her," Christine told *Rolling Stone* in 2022. "She and I are not competitive in any way at all. We're totally different, but totally sympathetic with each other. We are dear, dear friends. We don't have any competition onstage. She is who she is. I am who I am. Easy, easy, easy.

"I'm a tomboy, hanging out with the guys," she continued. "I love men. I love hanging around with men. And Stevie is kind of a girly-girl. She loves hanging out with her girlfriends."

The feeling was mutual. Stevie admired Christine's no-BS Britishness and looked to the keyboardist as a friend and mentor. "Christine very willingly gave me the stage, which I thought was very cool for a woman to say, 'Oh, she's . . . younger than me, and I've worked for ten years on the road, killed myself, and here she is, our new frontwoman,'" Stevie later recounted in the 2016 volume *Fleetwood Mac on Fleetwood Mac: Interviews and Encounters*. Meanwhile, Christine deeply appreciated Stevie's sense of humor, telling *The Guardian,* "It was critical that I got on with [Stevie]. Because I'd never played with another girl. But I liked her instantly. She was funny and nice, but also there was no competition. We were completely different on the stage to each other, and we wrote differently, too."

"We had to end up being close," Stevie also told *Uncut*. "Because otherwise it was just hang out with the guys all the time. . . . We are totally different, at complete opposite ends of the personality spectrum. The one thing we had in common, which bound us together, was a sense of humor through all the pain."

Forging a positive relationship with another woman wasn't a big ask for Stevie, who became known for always having an entourage of women around her after joining Fleetwood Mac. As Stephen Davis's *Gold Dust Woman* outlined, "Stevie's girls—Robin Snyder, Mary Torrey, Christie Alsbury, and others—dressed like Stevie, in long skirts and long hair with lots of accessories and drop-dead shades. They smelled like her, too, redolent of patchouli oil and sandalwood. They basically controlled access to Stevie and styled themselves as ladies-in-waiting to a virgin queen, making sure that Stevie felt supported and had what she needed in the studio."

Stevie wrote female solidarity into song, too, on the eerie *Tusk* rocker "Sisters of the Moon," which, as she later revealed to Jim Ladd, was an anxious reflection on her deteriorating health while on tour. "I walked out in front of the mirror and looked at myself and I was sick. . . . [The lyric] 'intense silence as she walked in the room' was me looking at myself. 'And the people they love her,' that's after the gigs; there are a million people and you're being pulled every way."

Though Stevie was far from perfect in her female relationships—she famously gave Lindsey's partner Carol Ann Harris the cold shoulder—the singer set a positive example when it came to camaraderie with other women in the industry. Much later, in late 2024, Stevie elaborated on her peaceable outlook to *Rolling Stone* while remembering a conversation she'd had with the pop star Katy Perry, who was talking about internet fan armies. "I hate it," Stevie said about internet-born fandom and rivalries. "About ten years ago, Katy Perry was talking to me about the internet armies of all the girl singers, and how cruel and rancid they were. I said, 'Well, I wouldn't know because I'm not on the internet.'"

This apparently was an alien concept for Perry. "She said, 'So, who are your rivals?'" Stevie continued. "I just looked at her. It was my steely look. I said, 'Katy, I don't have rivals. I have friends. All the other women singers that I know are friends. Nobody's competing. Get off the internet and you won't have rivals either.'"

Stevie's philosophy of friendship didn't just have the good fortune to materialize before the internet, social media, and pop music's warring fan armies. Many of her dearest friends have been in her life for decades, and it's been rare to hear of her falling out with anyone (save for Lindsey, for obvious reasons, and Sara Recor, though they eventually found their way back to each other). Stevie's even maintained friendships with former lovers—from Mick Fleetwood to Don Henley, both of whom she continued to creatively collaborate with.

Speaking of creative collaborations, one of Stevie's most enduring friendships was the one she had with Tom Petty. Stevie quickly fell in love with Tom's unique and down-to-earth blend of heartland rock and blues that reflected both his upbringing in Florida and his ambitious move to Los Angeles. She was equally taken with how his band, the Heartbreakers, filled out the group's sound, with Benmont Tench's harmonizing keys and Mike Campbell's jangling guitar. What's more, she recognized a sonic overlap with her own band. Stevie made it her mission to get Tom to contribute in some way to—maybe produce?—her debut solo album, *Bella Donna*. She flooded his management with calls, which initially went unanswered. "If I can't be in Tom Petty and the Heartbreakers, I want to make a record that sounds as much like T.P.'s as possible," she told her new manager, Irving Azoff, who swore he'd get Stevie anything and everything Petty-related that she wanted.

"Tom had the same influences we had," Stevie said. "The Byrds, Neil Young, Crosby, Stills and Nash—but he dropped in a lot of serious old blues. And Tom is such a great singer and so charismatic onstage. I became such a fan that if I hadn't been in a band myself, I would have joined that one."

When they finally connected in 1978, Tom was flattered—but suspicious. He and the Heartbreakers saw Fleetwood Mac as "this big, corporate rock band" and Stevie as this "larger-than-life star" with a too-Hollywood entourage, as he told Paul Zollo in the book *Conversations with Tom Petty.* "They were actually artistic people, but in those days, nobody trusted that sort of thing. We kept thinking, 'What does she want from us?'"

Tom eventually agreed to produce one song ("Outside the Rain") for Stevie, who he thought had a wonderful voice. After the trial track, he ultimately opted not to produce her solo album—he just couldn't get past Stevie's tendency to fill the studio with her girlfriends. Instead, he directed Stevie to his and the Heartbreakers' producer, Jimmy Iovine, who'd also worked with Patti Smith, John Lennon, and Bruce Springsteen. Under Jimmy's hard-line, work-comes-first stewardship, Stevie adopted a more focused attitude in the studio for *Bella Donna,* which also featured Benmont Tench as its musical director and old friend Waddy Wachtel, a session musician who'd played with Stevie and Lindsey on *Buckingham Nicks* and on the Fleetwood Mac track "Sugar Daddy."

Also in the studio for constant support: Robin (offering vocal coaching and occasional bumps of cocaine for energy) and Lori Perry-Nicks and Sharon Celani—Stevie's friends and backup singers, whose echoing vocals were heavily featured on "Edge of Seventeen." "They make my life easier," Stevie said of Lori and Sharon. "If I get tired and drop out, they pick it up for me. If I don't want to sing alone when I'm recording, then one of them just quietly sings along, smiles, and acts happy. I have to have people around me that love to sing and work, otherwise I feel like Alice in Wonderland because I don't relate to anybody, and nobody relates to me."

Lori, who married Stevie's brother, Christopher, in 1989, and Sharon have continued to work with Stevie on every solo album since *Bella Donna*. "My relationship with the girls is simple," Stevie said on *In Your Dreams*. "I could have had different background singers on every record I've ever done. I could have been a chameleon like Madonna. I could've hired anybody. But I didn't want to change. I think that my audience and my fans find comfort in the fact that Lori, Sharon, and I are very loyal to each other. I love the way they sing. I love the way they sound. I love how we sound together. I love the fact that they're innovative. I love the fact that they're here. . . . The world hears that friendship, and they find comfort in that love that we have as three very strong women that have come a long way together."

Stevie felt so appreciative of the team around her that she had a bunch of "very Rhiannon" 24-karat-gold crescent moon pendants made for everyone to wear—except for the Brooklyn-born Jimmy Iovine, who declared that he was *not* very Rhiannon.

Even if he wasn't "very Rhiannon," Jimmy had other things to contribute, like badgering Tom Petty into writing a song for *Bella Donna*. But when Tom wrote "Insider," he liked it so much that he wound up keeping it for himself and putting it on *Hard Promises*. (Stevie still got to sing on "Insider" and the ballad "You Can Still Change Your Mind," cementing her place as an honorary Heartbreaker.)

"She started a campaign for me to write her a song, and I kept saying, 'No, I don't have time,'" Tom recalled in the 2007 documentary *Runnin' Down a Dream*. "And she said: 'Please, just write me a song.' So she wore me down. When you write for other people, you often write in their style. But the truth is if somebody comes to you looking for a song, they're really looking for something that sounds like you; they've got plenty of things that sound like them. She was more attracted to the bluesier music, because it was something she didn't do. So I wrote her a song called 'Insider.' I played it for Jimmy and he was just elated."

For *Bella Donna,* Tom had another song in mind to give to Stevie—a leftover from his *Hard Promises* sessions. That turned out to be the now iconic "Stop Draggin' My Heart Around"—an aching, uptempo blues-rock duet between Stevie and Tom, who traded lovelorn verses over Mike Campbell's whining guitar. "We'd already cut it as a Heartbreakers song, with Tom singing the whole thing," Benmont Tench said. "At the same time, Jimmy Iovine was dating Stevie, though he was keeping it clandestine. And I think Jimmy thought the song could be a hit for her."

Credited to "Stevie Nicks with Tom Petty and the Heartbreakers," "Stop Draggin' My Heart Around" became an instant smash, peaking at number 3 on the *Billboard* Hot 100 and raising Stevie's profile as the next great female rock singer.

The press assumed that Stevie and Tom must also be secret lovers, which they never were. Stevie was firmly in a relationship with Jimmy by that point. But even if she had been single, she certainly never had any romantic designs on Tom. For one, she'd become good friends with his wife, Jane, and she liked that her collaborations with Tom were totally unclouded by romance, unlike her previous creative partnership with Lindsey Buckingham. "Tom and I aren't in love with each other, or haven't been in and out of love," she told *BAM* magazine. "We're just good friends, so we probably could write together. Lindsey and I have so much behind us that it would be difficult to sit down and get into lyrics. As it is, he asks me, 'Who's that one about? What are you talking about in that line? What does that mean?'"

Now, that isn't to say Stevie wouldn't have welcomed a romantic overture from Tom. As many have pointed out, the duet she wrote while on tour with Tom and Bob Dylan (later recorded with Bruce Hornsby), "Two Kinds of Love," has some pretty telling lyrics, which describe a "famous friend" who is also a "great temptation." Make of that what you will.

Also important: Tom was able to call Stevie out. To him, she was like a batty little sister, someone who could take him out of his often depressive mindset, while he was more like an anchor, bringing her back down to earth when necessary. "He'll say I'm like a plane without any radar," Stevie said. "He says to me, 'You're not living in the real world,' and I'm

I could have had different background singers on every record I've ever done. I could have been a chameleon like Madonna: I could've hired anybody. But I didn't want to change. I think that my audience and my fans find comfort in the fact that Lori, Sharon, and I are very loyal to each other. I love the way they sing. I love the way they sound. I love how we sound together. I love the fact that they're innovative. I love the fact that they're here.... The world hears that friendship, and they find comfort in that love that we have as three very strong women that have come a long way together.

saying, 'Are you living in the real world?' and he's going, 'Well, I live in more of a real world than you do, for sure.'"

Fortunately for everyone, after the remarkable success of "Stop Draggin'" and *Bella Donna,* Stevie and Tom would go on to have one of the most profound and rewarding friendships in rock history. When Stevie started ideating what would become *The Wild Heart,* she brought Tom, Benmont, and Mike back, as well as previous *Bella Donna* contributors Jimmy, Waddy, Sharon, Lori, Roy Bittan, and Don Felder. Still reeling from losing Robin, Stevie felt it was crucial that she circle the wagons if she was going to make it through recording her sophomore solo release. Tom contributed another duet, the mid-tempo ballad "I Will Run to You," which again featured Benmont on keys and Mike on guitar.

"Tom and I love to sing together," Stevie said of her latest Petty collab. "I'm not really very interested in developing relationships with other men singers, because this is just perfect: We sing well, we have a great time, we complement each other. I love his songwriting, perfect, why bother? Whatever the hassles that be that make it difficult—and believe you me, the hassles that be are everywhere to stop Tom and I from ever doing anything together—my relationship with him is more important. Anyway, the song's fabulous. It's beautiful, and I'm very honored that he even cared enough to write it for me."

Stevie's friendship with Tom created a new pathway to living out her rock star fantasies beyond what she could do on her own or with Fleetwood Mac. In 1986, Stevie took off to Australia to hang out with Tom on his True Confessions tour with the great Bob Dylan. While she'd appear onstage to help with backing vocals, on their Sydney tour stop Tom brought her back out for the set's encore of "Knockin' on Heaven's Door." "Tom knew it was going to be wonderful," Stevie later told Jim Ladd. "They both motioned over to me to sing on 'Knockin' on Heaven's Door,' so I did. In the next chorus, [Bob] turned to me and let me sing the choruses by myself.

"It was incredible. There's no way to explain what it would be like to someone like me, who went to Woodstock and decided that was what I wanted to do. . . . To stand on-stage with Bob Dylan and Tom Petty, it makes everything else that goes on that I don't love that much worth it."

The more time Stevie spent with Tom and his creative circle, the more opportunities for collaboration showed up that spanned well beyond just the Heartbreakers. In the mid-1980s, Stevie was interested in exploring a more synth-based pop sound, an aesthetic that had exploded in popularity and sent rock's old guard spinning out over the viability of guitar music. As Stevie started thinking about her third solo album, *Rock a Little,* she went back to Tom to see if he had any songs for her. This time, he didn't. But he knew someone who might. His buddy and neighbor Dave Stewart, who'd been a major contributor to the Heartbreakers' 1985 album, *Southern Accents.*

Dave and his Eurythmics musical partner, Annie Lennox, had taken over the charts that decade with dramatic synth-pop juggernauts like "Sweet Dreams (Are Made of This)" and "Here Comes the Rain Again." Dave and Stevie also had some personal details in common, namely that they'd both been in tumultuous romantic relationships with creative partners (Stevie with Lindsey, Dave with Annie) and broken up while keeping the band together.

Stevie first met Dave in a mideighties tornado of cocaine and lover's rage. After a Eurythmics gig at the Wiltern, he headed over to Stevie's for a party. They commiserated over their breakups; Dave had recently split with Annie, and Stevie had just gotten in a huge fight with then boyfriend Joe Walsh. Dave and Stevie spent the night together. In the morning, she asked him to kindly get up and get out of her house.

This is where details get a little fuzzy. Books like *Gold Dust Woman* and *Visions, Dreams, and Rumours* peg "Don't Come Around Here No More" as something Stevie told Dave the morning after their tryst. Meanwhile, the internet is convinced that Dave overheard Stevie shouting those words to Joe Walsh the next morning. His own memoir doesn't do much to clear this up, though it alludes to Stevie's rushing him out the door because "someone" might be stopping by to collect their things: "I was woken up at about 9:30 A.M. by Stevie saying I had to leave because someone might have been coming around to collect their clothes, and things could get tricky. I didn't like the sound of 'tricky,' so I phoned my management, found out where the band was staying, and jumped in a cab."

Whatever the actual origin of "Don't Come Around Here No More," Dave knew he had something and started writing it into a song for Stevie. But, as Stevie later recalled to VH1 about the song's history, she ended up storming out of the studio and tossed the track over to Tom. "We all went in the studio with me and David and Tom Petty. And the next day I came in and Tom had done the vocal on it. And because I was extremely selfish and spoiled rotten, I got very angry and fired everybody and stormed out. I told Tom to keep the song, said 'Thank you, David,' and left."

But as the eighties moved into the nineties, Stevie's addiction to Klonopin grew more insidious. To make matters worse, after she exited rehab, Stevie was in a dark place when it came to her music. The media response to 1994's *Street Angel* was dire. By the midnineties, Stevie's ultrafeminine persona had roundly gone out of vogue; instead, the zeitgeist was embracing more outwardly tough women in rock, like Sonic Youth's perma-aloof Kim Gordon, or Hole's growling Courtney Love. "[Stevie's] child-woman personality has served her for 20 years," wrote Kara Manning in *Rolling Stone,* likening Stevie to a "little girl made helpless by uncaring men and by her own isolation." Manning concluded that it was "overdue for the doe-eyed innocent to get tough."

Fans were supportive of their hero on the Street Angel tour, but critics harshly zeroed in on Stevie's fuller figure. Stevie took solace in another friendship around this time. Dallas Taylor, a well-known session drummer who appeared on Crosby, Stills and Nash's 1969 debut, and their 1970 follow-up with Neil Young, *Déjà Vu,* had been by her side as she fought to detox from Klonopin at the Daniel Freeman Memorial Hospital in Venice Beach. Dallas had been through his own personal hell with drug addiction. Dallas was especially equipped to support Stevie as she went through the worst detox of her life; by the early 1990s, he'd become a professional addiction specialist and interventionist in California. But Dallas had not escaped his addiction journey unscathed; in 1989, he'd been diagnosed with liver disease. The following year, a bunch of his musician friends—including David Crosby, Stephen Stills, Graham Nash, Neil Young, Don Henley, and Eddie Van Halen—organized a benefit concert to pay for a liver transplant. "You're looking at someone that should not be here," Dallas told a crowd in Malibu in 1990 after receiving a successful liver transplant. "By all rights I should be dead and buried with my peers. My peer group are people like Jimi Hendrix, Janis Joplin, Keith Moon. These are all people that I partied with—famous, very sick rock and rollers."

Boarding a bus for her Street Angel tour, Stevie took "my friend the drummer" along for the ride. "It was the only time I ever went on a bus . . . right after rehab, and I was really fragile." Though she never mentioned Dallas by name, she did allude to him in the 2013 documentary *In Your Dreams,* reminiscing about how they'd "made out across the United States" on that tour bus. Their tryst might have been a "forbidden romance" (Dallas was married at the time to Betty Wyman; Stevie thanked the couple in her *Street Angel* liner notes), but it meant a lot to the singer at the time, so much so that she wrote it into "For What It's Worth," which eventually made it onto 2011's *In Your Dreams.* "I was really fragile and scared, and I should not have been on a big tour, which I was," Stevie said. "When you come out of rehab, they tell you, 'Don't do anything. You need to be careful. Don't get married, don't sell your house, don't do anything stupid, because you may not feel that way in a year.'

"[He] did save my life, because I was not ready for thousands and thousands and thousands of people sober."

Both Stevie and Dallas knew the romantic layer to their friendship would be short-lived. "It happened on the road, it was what it was, and it was beautiful. But it wouldn't have lasted off the road. And he knew that. He was wise enough to say that to me. . . . The whole love that surrounded that situation, I was so appreciative of it, because there's nothing more scary than walking on that stage in front of ten thousand people and thinking that you might not be good enough to do it anymore. . . . And he took that away. He saved my life." (Dallas died in 2015 due to complications of viral pneumonia and kidney disease.)

Despite having her spirits temporarily lifted by Dallas, by the end of the Street Angel tour, Stevie remained in a dark place. A failed album, a poorly reviewed tour, endless and unwelcome commentary about her body. Not to mention that she'd only just come out of rehab—detoxing from Klonopin was its own trauma. Now, she had to deliver one more album to fulfill her contract with Atlantic Records.

First, Stevie got to work by hunkering down at home, where she spent days drawing, writing, and walking on her treadmill. After she emerged to record demos, she reached out to Tom. Her old friend was playing nearby at the Ritz-Carlton. The pair met for dinner, and she spilled her guts out on the table. After everything—losing nearly a decade to Klonopin, her first flop album, a poorly received tour—she'd hit a wall of writer's block. Would Tom consider writing something for her?

Tom set Stevie straight immediately with a tough-love lecture. "He said, 'You know what? Everybody makes mistakes. You can't blame yourself for the Klonopin—you didn't go out on the streets looking for that. That's just a nasty thing that happened to you, so now get over it. You're upset 'cause you're twenty pounds overweight—lose it, you can do it. That's not your problem.

" 'Your problem is knowing and remembering that you're a great songwriter. I'm not going to help you write songs, I don't have to help you. You need to go home to your piano and sit down and do what you love to do. You never married, you never had children because your love is songwriting, and what in the world is up with you telling me that you need me to help you write songs?'"

Tom's bluntness couldn't have gone down easy. If anyone else had said that to her, she might have gotten up and walked out. But this was Tom, and his snap-out-of-it lecture proved to be just the "kick in the butt" Stevie needed. Tom's words of wisdom became the inspiration for the song "That Made Me Stronger," which would eventually appear on Stevie's 2001 sixth studio album, *Trouble in Shangri-La.*

Fast-forward a few years, in 2009 Stevie famously reconnected with Dave on Fleetwood Mac's Unleashed tour stop in London. The two old friends talked for hours. Dave wondered if Stevie would play something for him on the piano, and she broke out a fifteen-minute rendition of "Rhiannon." "Then Dave joined in as if we'd been singing it together for years," Stevie recalled. "I realized then that if I ever were to make a solo album again—and believe me, I had my doubts—but if that day came, I knew I wanted to have Dave on board."

Stevie's vision morphed into reality the following year. Not only did Dave want to produce what would become *In Your Dreams,* but could they also film a documentary of the album's making in Stevie's home? As they started work together, Stevie brought out her dozens of poetry books and journals for inspiration, and they were off. It was nice to see that, even now that she was squarely in her sixties, Stevie could be surprised. For most of her songwriting life, Stevie had worked solo. "I have never been interested in writing with anybody—not Lindsey, not anybody," she said. "And all of a sudden I could actually understand why Lennon and McCartney wrote together, or Rodgers and Hammerstein, or any of the great songwriting teams. I don't know a thousand chords, and Dave doesn't have a book of forty poems. When you put those two things together, you have this amazing amount of wisdom and knowledge. Those five minutes when it all started was a brilliant moment. Stars went off. When it was done, I said, 'Well, I'm a changed woman.' And then we just continued."

Stevie's first solo album since 2001's *Trouble in Shangri-La* was a resounding success, debuting at number 6 on the *Billboard* 200—Stevie's fifth Top 10 album on that chart. In the UK, *In Your Dreams* debuted and peaked at number 14 on the UK Albums chart, giving Stevie her fifth Top 20 album there. The accompanying documentary, on which Dave and Stevie shared director credits, was released with a limited theatrical run in April 2013 and earned a nomination for the Audience Award at the 2013 SXSW Film Festival. (As of this writing, the documentary is not available on streaming services, but DVDs are still floating around for purchase.)

In 2014, Stevie reunited with Dave yet again to record *24 Karat Gold: Songs from the Vault,* a collection of songs she'd held on to from over the years but never got around to recording. The pair holed up in Nashville and knocked the album out in two months. "Lindsey will love this album," she joked to *Rolling Stone* upon the album's release. "Half the songs are about him."

By summer 2017, Stevie had grown concerned about her old friend Tom Petty. The Heartbreaker was on his gargantuan fortieth anniversary tour, and the two had even shared a stage once more at London's Hyde Park, where they performed "Stop Draggin' My Heart Around." Though he was nursing a fractured hip, a case of emphysema, and knee issues, Tom insisted on not only continuing but completing the fifty-three-date jaunt. To manage the pain, Tom was taking several different opioid medications. In October 2017, one week after his final show at the Hollywood Bowl, Tom died of an accidental drug overdose. Stevie, his biggest fan, was devastated, though not all that surprised. She had noticed his condition at Hyde Park, including how he needed the crew to drive him around backstage in a golf cart.

For years after Tom's death, journalists would press Stevie for memories of her good friend Tom. When *Rolling Stone* asked what she thought made him capable of such empathy, despite his tough-guy Florida upbringing and leading a band that was more like "a gang," Stevie replied that Tom had spent much of his life surrounded by strong women, including both marriages (Tom married his second wife, Dana, in 2001) and two daughters. "The women around him pretty much went their own way, and he was good with that," Stevie said. "He gave me a lot of advice about stuff. He was the kind of person who said, 'Here's my advice. If you take it, great. If you don't, that's fine too.' He was never going to shake a finger in your face and make you feel bad if you didn't take his advice."

It took Stevie much longer, relatively speaking, to process another death. When Christine McVie died of a stroke and metastatic cancer in November 2022, Stevie was truly shaken. As she wrote in a social media statement, Stevie hadn't even been aware that her "best friend in the whole world" was sick. About a year and a half later, Stevie was back in Hyde Park, this time with her good friend Harry Styles, who joined her for a duet on "Stop Draggin' My Heart Around." As Harry held her hand, Stevie paid tribute to Fleetwood Mac's own Songbird on what would have been her eighty-first birthday.

"It's taken me all this time to try and be able to deal with this situation," she told the crowd. "One thing my mom used to say to me when I was little was . . . 'Stevie, when you're hurt you always run to the stage.' That's what I've been doing ever since Chris passed away, is running to the stage. The only people that have been able to help me to get over this has been all of you."

Few words can genuinely capture the profound meaning of friendship in Stevie's life. Today, Stevie ends every performance by singing "Landslide" dedicated to Christine, whose presence she says she can feel with her onstage. Behind her is a photomontage of the two women together, which Stevie can't look at, lest she burst into tears onstage. Around her neck is a gemstone made from a portion of Christine's ashes.

Stevie also continues to cement her close friendships with "Sisters of the Moon" gold crescent necklaces. Nearly fifty years after she began giving them out in 1977, Stevie to this day will give these friendship tokens to her nearest and dearest (recent recipients include Harry Styles, Taylor Swift, Vanessa Carlton, and the HAIM sisters). "Members of the coven—her 'Sisters of the Moon'—are told the moons are lucky charms and to pass them along to another in need, should the moment arise," wrote the *Los Angeles Times* in 2020. (Never break the chain, right?)

"They deserve to have a moon," Stevie said. "They deserve to have that inspiration and that little tip of my top hat to them to say 'I believe in you, and I think that you're amazing. So I'm telling you right now, you can have it all if you want it.'"

They deserve to have a moon. They deserve to have that inspiration and that little tip of my top hat to them to say "I believe in you, and I think that you're amazing. So I'm telling you right now, you can have it all if you want it."

LESSON SIXTEEN

BE A TEACHER

When something does happen to me, whether it's that movie or whether it's actually happened to me, I feel that it's my duty to actually share that with all of you guys. I want to immediately go to my desk and start writing about it. Because I want to be a teacher. I would love to teach a class anywhere.

—Stevie Nicks, NPR The Record/SXSW, 2013

If I didn't make it in the music business, I would've been a teacher; I would have taken my music into the classroom somehow, and I would have figured out a way to use my writing and my music as a way to teach kids.

—Stevie Nicks, 2011

In the spring of 2013, Stevie Nicks filmed a forty-minute *Oprah's Master Class* interview covering nearly every stage of her life. The series format focused on interviewing legendary household names spanning music, entertainment, sports, media, and business about how they'd achieved success. Among the personalities interviewed were Jane Fonda, Sidney Poitier, Reba McEntire, Goldie Hawn, James Taylor, and Jeff Bridges—people who really need no introduction. People who've been everywhere, met everyone, and now have reams of wisdom to impart. Stevie's interview, which ran on *Master Class*'s third season and covered her career wins, errors in judgment, and lessons learned, is frequently quoted in just about every account of her life, including this one.

While Stevie's *Master Class* is a genuinely lovely interview, in looking back at the whole of her life, Stevie is candid and utterly matter-of-fact about any wrong turns she's taken while unabashedly celebrating herself. Near the end, she cites a letter she wrote to her father in 1973 talking about how recording *Buckingham Nicks* was going and seemingly predicting her own future: *Someday when I'm sitting in Beverly Hills in my small but beautiful house next to my small but elegant pool in my long, white cotton skirt and blouse with my hat, and enjoying all of the music that I love . . .*

"I planned it out!" Stevie laughs. "I think that my life is a testament to believing that if you want something, you can make it happen. . . . It's possible. I think what you just have to tell people is, it's all possible."

While she held a crystal vision of her life fifty years from then, it's worth wondering if the Stevie Nicks of 1973—a girl who struggled to be taken seriously as an artist and professional from under the more "legitimate" shadow of her guitar virtuoso boyfriend—could have predicted the ways she'd become a mentor and teacher to younger generations.

One of the reasons Stevie has yet to pen a memoir herself is because she feels she's already done exactly that within her songs. ("The world is not ready for my memoir, I guarantee you," she's joked.) Ultrapersonal songs like "Gold Dust Woman," "Silver Springs," and "Landslide" have set such a standard for truth telling in pop music that an artist of Stevie's stature could afford to cocoon herself away forever in that small yet elegant house. She could pull a Beyoncé and never speak to any journalist ever again if she chose. But Stevie will never be done telling her story, because there are always new lessons to impart.

In spring 2025, Stevie announced she was working on her first new album in fourteen years, and that this one would be her most personal volume yet. "I have seven songs, and they are autobiographical, real stories where I'm not pulling any punches for probably the first time in my life," she said. "They are not airy-fairy songs that you are wondering who they're about but you don't really get it. They're real stories of memories of mine, of fantastic men."

Any student of Stevie's music could argue that most of her songs are already varying degrees of autobiographical. What's evolved, however, is Stevie's awareness of her autobiographical writing—and how best to direct it.

At first, diaristic writing was just something Stevie *did* without thinking. On the raw and urgent *Rumours* closer "Gold Dust Woman," Stevie struggled in real time to process the way her life had exploded practically overnight. Where there was once scarcity and part-time waitressing gigs there were now screaming fans and jam-packed touring schedules (and bumps of cocaine as needed in order to power through).

"Being in Fleetwood Mac was like being in the army," Stevie told VH1 in 1997. "It was like, 'You have to be there. You have to be there, and you have to be there as on time as you can be there. And even if there is nothing you have to do, you have to be there.' So 'Gold Dust Woman' was really my kind of symbolic look at somebody going through a bad relationship, and doing a lot of drugs, and trying to just make it—trying to live—you know, trying to get through it to the next thing."

Not everyone can directly relate to the toll of being in a popular band, but anyone can understand physical exhaustion. That's not unique. This is what Stevie has always excelled at as a songwriter: taking the personal and widening it to cover the universal. Out of those universalities come genuinely teachable moments.

It's tricky to say when, precisely, Stevie morphed into the wisdom-dispensing fairy godmother we know today. On one hand, she was always writing lessons on love, humanity, and the female rock star experience into her songs. But audiences beyond her and Fleetwood Mac's fandom started paying closer attention in what I can ballpark to be about the late nineties, which coincided with her kicking Klonopin and the twenty-year *Rumours* nostalgia cycle.

As Fleetwood Mac became more of a historical pop music artifact, Stevie had more public opportunities to go in depth. With distance came remarkable perspective, especially with a soap-operatic album like *Rumours,* which captured in dizzying detail the dynamics between two breaking-up couples—Christine and John McVie, Lindsey and Stevie—and a founding drummer (Mick) with his own problematic marriage thrown in the middle.

"Love affairs are timeless—I mean, they don't change," Stevie could tell viewers twenty years after her band's landmark album was released. "That's why these songs [on *Rumours*] are timeless, I think. And that's why they're timeless to me and that's why I can walk out on the stage today and still sing them . . . and still feel the same way as when I wrote them, because I can remember how I felt at that point, and I can remember the tears, and I can remember how hard it was for me to play 'Dreams' the first time, for the whole band, because I know it would probably really upset Lindsey, and probably really upset Chris and John, and probably really upset Mick and really upset me. And if I could even get through it, I'd be lucky."

I guess these are just
all my lost children
coming back into
my arms.

LESSON SEVENTEEN

YOU CAN BORROW FROM ME ANY TIME

Okay, so now I'm "Mama Rockstar." It's cool. Actually, it's great. I take pride in knowing that people have benefited from the road I've traveled.

—Stevie Nicks, Billboard, 2001

✦

I like to say a "fairy godmother" as opposed to a mom because I don't become their moms. They have moms. They don't need another mom, but maybe they need a fairy godmother.

—Stevie Nicks, Huffington Post, 2014

✦

All you ever need to be is kind.

While Stevie Nicks would probably be the first to admit that she hasn't always behaved perfectly—she's a human being, after all, one who spent decades in a famously unregulated, substance-filled creative industry—she has managed to consistently lead with kindness. Even when male journalists were mocking her spiritual tendencies (and, years later, her physical appearance), Stevie rarely took it as an excuse to lash out. If anything, Stevie would process her feelings by retreating inward, often holing up in her house to write, draw, and reflect.

At the turn of the century, a new generation of female pop/rock performers—ones who grew up on a diet of Fleetwood Mac and Stevie Nicks—started to take over the radio waves, magazine covers, and MTV airtime. When asked about their inspirations, Vanessa Carlton, Sheryl Crow, and Sarah McLachlan (among many others) answered without hesitation: Stevie Nicks! Sheryl and Sarah even contributed to Stevie's 2001 album, *Trouble in Shangri-La* (Sheryl co-produced five tracks), along with Natalie Maines of the Chicks and Macy Gray. In 2001, *Rolling Stone* asked Stevie if she now considered herself to be the "mother superior" for women in music.

"I do. I do. And it's a nice feeling—I certainly would have never gone out looking for that, but it seems to be coming to me. I guess these are just all my lost children coming back into my arms," Stevie replied.

Stevie met Sheryl in the midnineties, just after Sheryl's cool-girl hit "All I Wanna Do" took off. "From the second we met, I realized that we came from the same musical place," Stevie told the *Los Angeles Times*. "We both love harmony singing, the old folk music and old country music, besides our love for rock 'n' roll." In 2021, Sheryl told *Bustle* how Stevie was "my champion as a young artist, my role model as a kid from nine years old on."

As this book's chapter on friendship laid out in detail, Stevie has consistently been generous in platonic relationships, doling out gifts as symbols of cosmic connections. From the nineties on, however, Stevie's friendship with younger musicians evolved into full-on mentorship. Sheryl Crow, whom Stevie helped induct into the Rock and Roll Hall of Fame in 2023, is just one planet in a galaxy of relationships. To dig into all of them would probably require its own book. So let's focus on the highlights, beginning with another rising pop godmother: Taylor Swift.

Another lifetime admirer of Stevie's, Taylor got the chance to perform with Stevie early in her career. In 2010, the two performed "Rhiannon" and "You Belong with Me" at the 52nd Grammy Awards (Stevie harmonized on the latter, naturally). For context's sake, this might not be a live moment that Taylor likes to remember, as she was heavily criticized following their duet for singing off-key. "I had a bad night,"

Taylor admitted to *Rolling Stone* in 2012. "It's one of those things where you've rehearsed over and over and when the camera turns on, the nerves kick in and you just can't think straight." Honestly, understandable.

Stevie no doubt saw a lot of her younger self in Taylor's early career trajectory, which she touched on in a tribute in 2010's *TIME 100* issue, in which she praised the rising singer's ease at moving between genres and her overall ambition. "It's an innocence that's so special and so rare," Stevie wrote. "This girl writes the songs that make the whole world sing, like Neil Diamond or Elton John. She sings, she writes, she performs, she plays great guitar. Taylor can do ballads that could be considered pop or rock and then switch back into country. When I turned twenty years old, I had just made the serious decision to never be a dental assistant. Taylor just turned twenty, and she's won four Grammys."

When asked about her budding friendship with Stevie, Taylor (in 2010) marveled, "She has taught me some of the most important lessons. I feel like I made a new friend, sort of like this guardian angel-type person."

Years later, in June 2024, Stevie would attend Taylor's history-making Eras Tour in Dublin. That night, Taylor introduced her Nicks-referencing song "Clara Bow" with a speech about her friend Stevie, "who has really been one of the reasons why I—or any female artist—gets to do what we get to do."

Taylor added: "She's paved the way for us, and she's mentored so many artists that you don't even know she's doing it.

She's become friends with so many female artists just to be a guiding hand. I can't tell you how rare that is. She's a hero of mine and also someone that I can tell her any secret, and she'd never tell anybody. She's really helped me through so much over the years."

To this day, Stevie has been a source of wisdom and support for Taylor, who revealed in December 2025 during an appearance on *The Late Show with Stephen Colbert* that she calls Stevie for advice. "I have Stevie Nicks in my life in a way that affects me positively constantly," Taylor said. "Being able to talk with her and have a phone call with her and hear what she's been through . . . she paved the way for me and many other artists out there."

Objectively, it's easy to see how Stevie would be drawn to advising artists like Taylor and Sheryl Crow; all three women are blond and have straddled the lines between pop, rock, and country (recall that Stevie grew up singing the latter genre with her grandfather A.J.). But Stevie has been just as much of a mentor figure to younger musicians who land in a more alternative, experimental space. Take Lorde, for example.

"I think [Lorde is] just as odd as you or me," Stevie said during a 2022 conversation with *The New Yorker.* "She's a strange girl, and so are we. She's a really great writer, and she's really good at doing her own recorded stuff. I don't think that any real serious songwriter is ever going to have a problem staying connected to the dream world that allows us to write songs.

"We want to have our serious side and all that, but you can't take yourself too seriously," Stevie continued. "When you keep music in your life, I think it just changes you and pulls you out of a deep hole. [Lorde] just has to keep doing what she's doing."

Meanwhile, in November 2014, Stevie beamed down support to a SoCal sister trio from the Valley: Alana, Este, and Danielle Haim. When HAIM (today one of the premier rock acts in the world) were first gathering speed via breakthrough singles like "Falling" and "The Wire," critics loved to describe their harmony-heavy sound as being reminiscent of Fleetwood Mac, whom the sisters cited as a big influence. So when Fleetwood Mac played the LA Forum during their On with the Show tour, Stevie spoke directly to HAIM, who were sitting in the audience.

> Maybe twice in my lifetime I have met a group of other singers, artists, songwriters that I have thought were going to be a major force in rock and roll. And tonight, the ladies HAIM are here—Alana, Este, and Danielle. And I have to say, because I love sharing stuff with the audience about other people that I love—we've been on the road for twenty-seven shows, and I play their record [*Days Are Gone*] every day; I love it . . .
>
> It gives me answers, it gives me advice, it wraps its wings around me and it tells me everything will be okay, and I have such respect for them, and I have such respect

for who they are and how they play music and how they put their music together, and it just blows my mind.

So, girls, never stop. Don't stop thinking about tomorrow. Don't stop. Keep doing what you're doing because you're important to this world.

Truly, after a kind word from Stevie, contemporary pop stars tend to fall all over themselves as if they've been touched by an angel. Take Miley Cyrus for another example. Unlike Stevie, Miley (the daughter of country-pop behemoth Billy Ray Cyrus) has been famous pretty much since birth, acting and singing as Hannah Montana starting at age thirteen and releasing decades' worth of hit songs since then. But Miley and Stevie do have a few things in common: Both have struggled at points to be taken seriously by critics despite releasing wildly popular music, both have been treated cruelly by a sexist media machine, and both have displayed enormous strength through perseverance. Today, Miley is on her way to becoming another pop music godmother, dispensing wisdom to the generations that come after her.

It's strange to think Miley and Stevie weren't in touch prior to 2020, when Miley released her eighties-rock-inspired album *Plastic Hearts,* which sampled "Edge of Seventeen" on lead single "Midnight Sky." Upon reaching out to Stevie for permission to sample the shuddering guitar loop from "Edge of Seventeen," Miley not only got a yes from its author but also a personal letter. "I sent her the song, and I said, 'I have an alternate melody, if you don't want me to pay tribute to you and your greatness and how much you've inspired me,'" Miley said during a visit to *The Tonight Show*. "And she said, 'You can borrow from me any time.'

"I'm like, 'Shit, if you're feeling that way, can I just borrow, like, you and your time?'" she recalled. The pair's correspondence even led to the *Midnight Sky* remix of "Edge of Midnight" with Stevie recording new vocals. "That was one of the trippier experiences of my life—having my words come out of Stevie Nicks's mouth—because her words have come out of mine a billion times," Miley told *The Howard Stern Show* of the experience.

Stevie's friendship is not limited to only women, either. She is famously very close to former One Directioner turned solo artist Harry Styles, who helped induct her into the Rock and Roll Hall of Fame in 2019, calling Stevie "everything you've ever wanted in a lady, in a lover, in a friend." In turn, Stevie has poured out her feelings about Harry in interviews, calling him "the son she never had" and even her "love child" with Mick Fleetwood.

And finally, there's "Grandma Stevie."

Years after Robin Snyder Anderson's death, Stevie reconnected with her best friend's (now grown-up) son, Matthew, who now has a daughter of his own. Her name is Robin.

In an interview with *The Guardian* in 2020, Stevie talked about her relationship with "Little Robin," saying, "Last

Christmas, she was at my house and she comes into the kitchen, grabs my hand and goes: 'Come with me, Grandma Stevie,' and I'm going: 'Did this child just call me Grandma Stevie?' She did. . . . On that day I wrote in my journal, and it said: 'I promise you, Robin, that I will be Grandma Stevie until death does us part.'"

"Grandma Stevie" is just one of a few endearing nicknames (Nicksnames?) Stevie has collected in recent years. Natalie Maines of the Chicks has taken to calling her "Rock and Roll Mama." She has so many goddaughters, including Mick Fleetwood's twins Tessa and Ruby and Paul Fishkin's daughter Molly, she's practically lost count. (According to the *Los Angeles Times,* the number hovers at eleven or twelve.) One day, Stevie plans to leave her many journals to her goddaughters.

Even if Stevie had daughters of her own, she has said that biological motherhood wouldn't change her impulse to mentor younger generations. "I would still be doing this," she said. "I would still be looking around the music business or the arts business for people that I like and respect, that I think can carry on my tradition, which is just the tradition of simply being as great as you can be."

ACKNOWLEDGMENTS

Writing this book has been one of the most special experiences of my life. Spending hours a day immersed in the wisdom and knowledge of Stevie Nicks hardly ever felt like work; it was a privilege. I first want to thank my Harmony Books editor, Donna Loffredo, for approaching me with the idea for this book and trusting me to capture the spirit of Stevie Nicks in a new and profound way. I also want to thank the entire team at Harmony and Penguin Random House for their kindness, respect, communication, and utter professionalism. I feel wildly fortunate that this is the group I got to work with for what would be my first book. I hope we'll have the opportunity to work together on many others.

I also want to thank my amazing literary agent, Kara Rota, who has shepherded me through the opaque publishing process and thoughtfully answered all my questions, no matter how granular or inane I think they are before I hit "send" on the email draft.

To that end, I especially want to thank my friend Michael Tedder for introducing me to Kara, for inviting me to read on multiple occasions at his writers' meetup Words & Guitars, and for fostering such a lovely sense of community among creatives. Michael, I'm so glad to know you.

Speaking of people I'm grateful to know, I want to thank one of my all-time best friends and music industry colleagues Sarah Avrin. Sarah, when we first met over beers in Greenpoint more than ten years ago, I thought, "Not only is this chick rad as hell, but she might also be one of the most genuinely friendly people I've ever met. I hope she'll be my friend." Sarah, I love you to death, and I'm so happy to have you in my life. Thank you for your advice, publicity services, and for being my bestie even though I refuse to go hiking with you.

Thank you to John Kinney at The Nicks Fix (rockalittle.com) for archiving decades of interviews (magazine, newspaper, radio, internet, TV, more) with Stevie Nicks. The Nicks Fix was a massive resource for me as I wrote this book; I'm grateful to you for digitizing interviews that I'm pretty sure must reach into the thousands.

Thank you to the writers and editors at *Rolling Stone,* who have also made decades' worth of interviews with Stevie Nicks and the members of Fleetwood Mac available online. Additionally, thank you to Nicks biographers Stephen Davis and Zoë Howe: Your respective volumes on the Gold Dust Woman were fantastic resources in researching Stevie's life.

Thank you to the writers, editors, and friends who constantly inspire me with their work: Ilana Kaplan, Pamela Chelin, Caitlin Wolper, Maria Sherman, Hilary Hughes, Bonnie Stiernberg, Hilary Saunders, Annie Zaleski, Melissa Locker, Aviv Rubinstien, Nate Jackson, Mikael Wood, Eliza Berman, Kelly Conniff, Liz Garber-Paul, Maria Fontoura,

Marissa Muller, Brady Gerber, Philip Cosores, Dan Ozzi, Chris Molanphy, Justin Joseph, Chris Martins, Tommy West, Robbie Daw, the entire team at *Stereogum,* my former *SPIN* editors Kyle McGovern and Andrew Unterberger, Dawn Roode, and anyone else who has ever let me write for them.

Thank you to Debby, my sister and truest friend in the world. You would be my Sister of the Moon, even if we didn't share DNA.

Thank you to my high school English teacher Ellin Glassband, the first educator to take me aside and tell me that I was a good writer. Your encouragement meant more to me than you can possibly know. Thank you to the entire English department at my alma mater, Muhlenberg College, and in particular professors David Rosenwasser and Jill Stephen. Asking "So what that this is true?" will always guide my critical writing process.

Thank you to my parents, Charles and Karen Brodsky, who live their lives with purpose and meaning and have always inspired me to do the same. Thank you for encouraging my love of music and literature and never once making me feel like it was a risky move to declare an English major. Thank you for being my parents and thank you for being my friends.

Finally, thank you to my husband, Taylor. I will never have sufficient words to properly thank you for your unending love, support, and morning cups of coffee in bed. In the words of Stevie Nicks: *Unconditional love . . . / I'll be there when you fall / The one condition of love . . . / Is there are none at all.*

BIBLIOGRAPHY

Introduction

Steve Pond, "The US Interview: Stevie Nicks," *US* magazine, July 9–23, 1990, rockalittle.com/us1.htm.

Lesson One: Believe in Destiny

Jancee Dunn, "Women in Rock 2002: Stevie Nicks, at 54, Is Still the Coolest Chick in the Room," *Rolling Stone,* October 31, 2002, rollingstone.com/music/music-news/women-in-rock-2002-stevie-nicks-at-54-is-still-the-coolest-chick-in-the-room-197070/.

Steve Pond, "The US Interview: Stevie Nicks," *US* magazine, July 9–23, 1990, http://rockalittle.com/us1.htm.

"Parents Are Rocker Stevie Nicks' Biggest Fans," *Arizona Republic,* July 10, 2003, rockalittle.com/article_az_republican_july10_2003.htm.

Jenny Boyd, *It's Not Only Rock 'n' Roll: Iconic Musicians Reveal the Source of Their Creativity* (John Blake, 2013).

Michael Lyons, "Stevie Nicks: Arizona's Bella Donna Comes Home," *Arizona Living,* September 1983, rockalittle.com/article_arizona_living_sep_1983.htm.

Interview magazine, 1997, inherownwords.com/earlyyrs1.htm.

"Stevie Nicks Accepts the Icon Award at the 2014 BMI Pop Awards," youtube.com/watch?v=BjM-K5Zqq3g.

Mike Ragogna, "Chatting with Stevie Nicks," *Huffington Post,* October 4, 2012, fleetwoodmacnews.com/2012/10/in-your-dreams-conversation-with-stevie.html.

Alicia Kort, "Five Things You Might Not Know About Stevie Nicks," *Interview* magazine, November 14, 2017, interviewmagazine.com/music/five-things-might-not-know-stevie-nicks.

Liz Derringer, *High Times* magazine, March 1982, rockalittle.com/hightimes3-82.htm#:~:text=HIGH%20TIMES:%20Does%20that%20come,article%20to%20The%20Nicks%20Fix.

Simon Morrison, *Mirror in the Sky: The Life and Music of Stevie Nicks* (University of California Press, 2022).

Steven P. Wheeler, "Stevie Nicks: Rock's Street Angel," *Rokritr,* July 27, 2019, rokritr.com/2019/07/27/stevie-nicks-rocks-street-angel/.

Sheryl Crow, "With Her First Solo Album in Seven Years, Rock's Poetess Finds Her Life Is Rhyming Once Again," *Interview* magazine,

May 2001, https://www.fleetwoodmac-uk.com/articles/archive/SNart010.html.
Blair Jackson, "Stevie: Fleetwood Mac's Siren Soars with Her First Solo Album, Bella Donna," *BAM* magazine, September 11, 1981, angelfire.com/sc/stevienicks/stevienicks/STEVIE_NICKS_INTERVIEWS.
Cameron Crowe, "The True Life Confessions of Fleetwood Mac," *Rolling Stone,* March 24, 1977, rollingstone.com/feature/the-true-life-confessions-of-fleetwood-mac-120867/.
The Island Ear, August 22, 1994, inherownwords.com/earlyyrs2.htm.
James McNair, "Stevie Nicks Interviewed," *MOJO,* 2013. mojo4music.com/articles/stories/stevie-nicks-interviewed/.
Craig McLean, "Stevie Nicks Talks Addiction, Botox, and the Burying of Hatchets," *The Telegraph,* September 13, 2013, telegraph.co.uk/culture/music/rockandpopfeatures/10305143/Fleetwood-Macs-Stevie-Nicks-on-addiction-Botox-and-the-burying-of-hatchets-interview.html.
Helen Brown, "Stevie Nicks: The Most Fun I've Ever Had," *The Telegraph,* June 22, 2011, telegraph.co.uk/culture/music/music-festivals/8592526/Stevie-Nicks-The-most-fun-Ive-ever-had.html.
Sylvie Simmons, "The Q Interview: Stevie Nicks: 'I Had to Be Strong, Otherwise I Would Never Have Gotten Through All This,'" *Q* magazine, May 2008, rocksbackpages.com/Library/Article/the-iqi-interview-stevie-nicks-i-had-to-be-strong-otherwise-i-would-never-have-gotten-through-all-this.
Yuval Taylor, "The Ballad of Stevie Nicks and Lindsey Buckingham," *GQ,* October 2, 2025, gq.com/story/the-ballad-of-stevie-nicks-and-lindsey-buckingham.

Lesson Two: Go Fearlessly into the Dark

Rob Sheffield, "Stevie Nicks on Twirling, Kicking Drugs and a Lifetime with Lindsey," *Rolling Stone,* October 2, 2014, rollingstone.com/music/music-news/stevie-nicks-on-twirling-kicking-drugs-and-a-lifetime-with-lindsey-176143/.
Sheryl Crow, "With Her First Solo Album in Seven Years, Rock's Poetess Finds Her Life Is Rhyming Once Again," *Interview* magazine, May 2001, https://www.fleetwoodmac-uk.com/articles/archive/SNart010.html.
"Stevie Nicks & Sarah McLachlan," *Interview* magazine, March 1995, fleetwoodmac-uk.com/articles/archive/SNart011.html.
Cameron Crowe, "The True Life Confessions of Fleetwood Mac," *Rolling Stone,* March 24, 1977, https://www.rollingstone.com/feature/the-true-life-confessions-of-fleetwood-mac-120867/.

Blair Jackson, "Stevie: Fleetwood Mac's Siren Soars with Her First Solo Album, *Bella Donna*," *BAM* magazine, September 11, 1981, http://rockalittle.com/bam9-11-81.htm.
"Stevie Nicks: Blonde on Blonde," *SPIN* magazine, October 1997, fleetwoodmac-uk.com/articles/archive/SNart007.html.
Stephen Davis, *Gold Dust Woman: The Biography of Stevie Nicks* (St. Martin's Press, 2017).
James McNair, "Stevie Nicks Interviewed," *MOJO*, 2013. mojo4music.com/articles/stories/stevie-nicks-interviewed/.
Stevie Nicks, "Garbo" (Unaired VH1 Storytellers 1998 – Live & Rare), youtube.com/watch?v=3rzEOrWHu3Q.
Stevie Nicks, *Enchanted: The Works of Stevie Nicks* (Box Set), 1998.
Brian Hiatt, "Stevie Nicks: A Rock Goddess Looks Back," *Rolling Stone*, January 29, 2015, rollingstone.com/music/music-news/stevie-nicks-a-rock-goddess-looks-back-179984/.
Stephen Davis, *Gold Dust Woman: The Biography of Stevie Nicks* (St. Martin's Press, 2017).
Craig McLean, "Stevie Nicks: The Men, the Music, the Menopause," *The Guardian*, March 25, 2011, theguardian.com/music/2011/mar/25/stevie-nicks-interview.

Lesson Three: Tell the Truth, Always

Stevie Nicks Australia Interview, 2011, youtube.com/watch?v=cggawhco1N4.
Mark Goodman, Faces Interview of the Month, MTV (1983), rockalittle.com/interview_mtv_1983.htm.
CNN Interview, 1989, tiktok.com/@stevienxksfix/video/7478801284770975007.
Mick Fleetwood, *Play On: Now, Then & Fleetwood Mac: The Autobiography* (Little, Brown, 2014).
Timothy White, *Billboard* magazine, 1998, inherownwords.com/longdistance.htm.
Adrian Thrills, "On the Eve of Fleetwood Mac's Reunion, Stevie Nicks Tells How Their Wild Past Still Inspires Them," *Daily Mail*, October 16, 2009, dailymail.co.uk/tvshowbiz/article-1220747/On-eve-Fleetwood-Macs-reunion-Stevie-Nicks-tells-wild-past-inspires-them.html.
Performer Songwriter magazine, 2003, inherownwords.com/landslide.htm.
Rolling Stone, 1977.
Anna Kaplan, "Stevie Nicks on Her Own Barbie, Advice to Taylor Swift and Why Her Retirement Plans Involve a Wolfhound," TODAY.com,

October 1, 2023, today.com/popculture/music/stevie-nicks-barbie-taylor-swift-retirement-plans-rcna117449.

Lesson Four: Believe in Crystal Visions

Stevie Nicks, VH1 Storytellers, 1998.

Walter Berry, "Stevie Nicks Sees the World in a Blur," Associated Press, August 11, 1983, stevienicks.info/1983/08/11/stevie-nicks-sees-world-in-a-blur/.

Cameron Crowe, "Joni Mitchell: 'I Don't Feel Guilty for My Success or My Lifestyle,'" *Rolling Stone,* July 26, 1979, rollingstone.com/feature/joni-mitchell-defends-herself-61890/.

Mary Bartlet Leader, *Triad: A Novel of the Supernatural* (Coward, McCann & Geoghegan, 1973).

Stevie Nicks, "In the Studio with Fleetwood Mac," www3.rocktrop, inherownwords.com/dreams.htm.

Timothy White, "Stevie Nicks' Magic Act," *Rolling Stone,* September 3, 1981, rollingstone.com/music/music-news/stevie-nicks-magic-act-242776/.

Jeff Giles, "When Stevie Nicks Got Introspective on 'The Other Side of the Mirror,'" *Ultimate Classic Rock,* May 11, 2014, ultimateclassicrock.com/stevie-nicks-other-side-of-mirror/.

Amy Kaufman, "The Moonlight Confessions of Stevie Nicks," *Los Angeles Times,* September 30, 2020, latimes.com/entertainment-arts/music/story/2020-09-30/stevie-nicks-fleetwood-mac-solo-concert-film.

Andrea Dresdale, "The Year in Music: Stevie Nicks' 2020 Was a 'Dreams' Come True," ABC Audio, December 30, 2020, 1450wnby.com/2020/12/30/the-year-in-music-stevie-nicks-2020-was-a-dreams-come-true/.

Daisann McLane, "Five Not So Easy Pieces: Fleetwood Mac Is More than the Sum of Its Parts," *Rolling Stone,* 1980, rockalittle.com/rs_issue310.htm.

Lesson Five: Live in a World of Magic

Robert Henschen, "Stevie Nicks Does Magic Tricks: Mac's Sorceress Now Casts a Solo Spell," *US* magazine, October 28, 1980, rockalittle.com/us10-28-80.htm.

Chris Salewicz, "Fleetwood Mac: Can't Go Home Again," *New Musical Express,* 1980, stevienicks.info/1980/04/01/fleetwood-mac-cant-go-home-again/.

Stevie Nicks, *Crawdaddy* magazine, November 1976, inherownwords.com/rhiannon.htm.

Lester Bangs, *Creem* magazine (1977).
"Stevie Nicks Denies Witch Rumor," Associated Press, May 30, 1998, rockalittle.com/notwitch.htm.
Yvonne Villarreal, "Stevie Nicks Talks 'American Horror Story': 'I Was Scared to Go There,'" *Los Angeles Times,* January 8, 2014, latimes.com/entertainment/tv/showtracker/la-et-st-stevie-nicks-american-horror-story-20140107-story.html.
Larry Flick, "Stevie Nicks Returns with Sheryl Crow in Tow," *Billboard* magazine, February 12, 2001.
Stevie Nicks, "Stevie Nicks: Gold Dust Woman Returns," VH1.com, April 1, 2001.
Danny Goldberg, *Bumping into Geniuses: My Life Inside the Rock and Roll Business* (Penguin, 2008).
Stephen Davis, *Gold Dust Woman: The Biography of Stevie Nicks* (St. Martin's Press, 2017).
Jim Ladd, "Fleetwood Mac—*Tusk* Interview" (1979), inherownwords.com/witches.htm.
Mark Goodman, "Stevie: Wild Angel on the Wing," Faces Interview of the Month, MTV (1983), rockalittle.com/interview_mtv_1983.htm.
Denise Martin, "Stevie Nicks Talks Twirling, Shawls, and Playing American Horror Story's White Witch," *Vulture,* January 8, 2014, vulture.com/2014/01/stevie-nicks-american-horror-story-interview.html.

Lesson Six: Float In Like Goddesses

"Stevie Nicks: Blonde on Blonde," *SPIN* magazine, October 1997.
Glamour, 1981, inherownwords.com/image.htm.
Chad Swiatecki, "SXSW Interview: Stevie Nicks," *Austin American-Statesman,* March 14, 2013, stevienicks.info/2013/03/14/sxsw-interview-stevie-nicks/.
Ann Powers, "Stevie Nicks: 'When We Walk Into the Room, We Have to Float In Like Goddesses,'" NPR, March 17, 2013, npr.org/sections/therecord/2013/03/17/174494011/stevie-nicks-when-we-walk-into-the-room-we-have-to-float-in-like-goddessses.
Ruth La Ferla, "Still Dressing for Stevie," *The New York Times,* April 8, 2009, nytimes.com/2009/04/09/fashion/09STEVIE.html.
Stevie Nicks Interview, YouTube Archival Video (1986), youtube.com/watch?v=aQV_N_SJA64.
Stevie Nicks, Backstage Prep Video YouTube (1970s), youtube.com/watch?v=wAekACkue6U.
High Times magazine (1982), http://www.inherownwords.com/image.htm.

Jacob Bernstein, "Nick of Time: Q&A with Stevie Nicks," *WWD,* March 31, 2009, wwd.com/eye/people/nick-of-time-qa-with-stevie-nicks-2087768/?changecurrentdate=true&date=2009-03-31&save_in_session=true#/articlehttp://www.wwd.com/lifestyle-news/nick-of-time-qa-with-stevie-nicks-2087768?page=1.

Lesson Seven: Don't Be Sorry for Anything

Samantha Leach, "Stevie Nicks on Her Career, Love Life," *Bustle,* November 11, 2020, stevienicks.info/2020/11/04/stevie-nicks-on-tiktok-tom-petty-claiming-whats-yours/.

Joe Benson, "Off the Record with Stevie Nicks," The Sound 100.3 FM (1990s), rockalittle.com/offtherecord.htm.

Joe Taysom, "The Poignant Advice Stevie Nicks Would Give to Her Younger Self," *Far Out* magazine, July 28, 2023, faroutmagazine.co.uk/the-poignant-advice-stevie-nicks-would-give-to-her-younger-self/.

Nigel Williamson, "Fleetwood Mac: 'Everybody Was Pretty Weirded Out'—the Story of Rumours," *Uncut* magazine, May 2003, uncut.co.uk/features/fleetwood-mac-everybody-was-pretty-weirded-out-the-story-of-rumours-26395/.

Mick Fleetwood, *Play On: Now, Then & Fleetwood Mac: The Autobiography* (Little, Brown, 2014).

Jenny Boyd, *It's Not Only Rock 'n' Roll: Iconic Musicians Reveal the Source of Their Creativity* (John Blake, 2013).

Simon Price, "Stevie Nicks: 'Love Is Fleeting for Me . . . in My Life as a Travelling Woman,'" *The Independent,* June 26, 2011, stevienicks.info/2011/06/26/stevie-nicks-love-is-fleeting-for-me-in-my-life-as-a-travelling-woman/.

Bailey Richards, "The Story of Stevie Nicks' 'Silver Springs': 'Probably the Best Song I've Ever Written,'" *People* magazine, October 2, 2023, people.com/stevie-nicks-silver-springs-the-story-of-the-fleetwood-mac-track-7975700.

Leah Greenblatt, "Stevie Nicks on Her Favorite Songs," *Entertainment Weekly,* March 31, 2009, fleetwoodmacnews.com/2009/03/ew-stevie-nicks-on-her-favorite-songs.html.

Timothy White, "Stevie Nicks' Magic Act," *Rolling Stone,* September 3, 1981, rollingstone.com/music/music-news/stevie-nicks-magic-act-242776/

Charlotte Heathcote, "Stevie Nicks Is Going Her Own Way," *Sunday Express UK,* October 18, 2009, fleetwoodmacnews.com/2009/10/stevie-nicks-is-going-her-own-way.html.

24 Karat Gold—Songs from the Vault, Facebook Q&A, November 5, 2014, stevienicks.info/2014/11/05/stevie-answers-your-questions-on-facebook/.

BAM magazine, August 22, 1997, inherownwords.com/lindsey2.htm.

Lesson Eight: Do Something Creative Every Day

The Island Ear, August 22, 1994, inherownwords.com/writing.htm.

Jenny Boyd, *Musicians in Tune: 75 Contemporary Musicians Discuss the Creative Process* (Fireside, 1992).

Blair Jackson, "Stevie: Fleetwood Mac's Siren Soars with Her First Solo Album, Bella Donna," *BAM* magazine, September 11, 1981.

Denver Post, August 12, 1991, inherownwords.com/writing.htm.

Baltimore Sun, July 25, 1991, inherownwords.com/writing.htm.

"Eye to Eye: Stevie Nicks on Songwriting," *CBS Sunday Morning* (2007), youtube.com/watch?v=KIlfT-aDTko.

Lesson Nine: Look to Your Guardian Angels

Stevie Nicks, "Dear All Armed Forces Members," *The Nicks Fix* (2004), rockalittle.com/thanksgiving2004.htm.

Rockline (radio interview), ABC Studios (1989), stevienicks.info/music/stevie-nicks-the-other-side-of-the-mirror-1989/ghosts/.

Angie Martoccio, "Stevie Nicks: I Believe in the Church of Stevie," *Rolling Stone,* October 24, 2024, rollingstone.com/music/music-features/stevie-nicks-fleetwood-mac-kamala-harris-new-music-1235140437/.

Stephen Davis, *Gold Dust Woman: The Biography of Stevie Nicks* (St. Martin's Press, 2017).

Timothy White, "Music to My Ears: Atlantic Honors Stevie Nicks with Lavish 3-CD 'Enchanted' Anthology," *Billboard* magazine, April 18, 1998, rockalittle.com/billbrd3.htm.

Interview magazine, July 1998, inherownwords.com/witches.htm.

"Stevie Nicks' Devastating Loss and Life-Changing Advice," *Oprah's Master Class,* OWN (2013), youtube.com/watch?v=ohPGQ6AEdoI.

Jenny Stevens, "Stevie Nicks on Art, Ageing and Attraction: 'Botox Makes It Look Like You're in a Satanic Cult!,'" *The Guardian,* October 14, 2020, theguardian.com/music/2020/oct/14/stevie-nicks-on-art-ageing-and-attraction-botox-makes-it-look-like-youre-in-a-satanic-cult.

Amy Kaufman, "The Moonlight Confessions of Stevie Nicks," *Los Angeles Times,* September 30, 2020.

Stevie Nicks, MusiCares Person of the Year Acceptance Speech (2018), youtube.com/watch?v=WM_Wonk4CNM.

Chris Willman, "Stevie Nicks on Her New Concert Film, the 'Crazy' Resurgence of 'Dreams' and Staying in Touch with the Spirits of Prince and Tom Petty," *Variety,* October 25, 2020, variety.com/2020/music/news/stevie-nicks-24-karat-gold-concert-film-interview-1234815282/.

Lesson Ten: Be a Totally Free Woman

Jada Yuan, "Stevie Nicks, the Fairy Godmother of Rock," *Vulture,* June 9, 2013, vulture.com/2013/06/stevie-nicks-on-life-at-65-with-fleetwood-mac.html.

Joan Anderman, "Stevie Nicks, Just Following Her Muse," *New York Times,* February 4, 2014, nytimes.com/2014/02/04/booming/stevie-nicks-just-following-her-muse.html.

Jon Blistein, "Stevie Nicks Recalls Split with Lindsey Buckingham," *Rolling Stone,* March 21, 2013, rollingstone.com/music/music-news/stevie-nicks-recalls-split-with-lindsey-buckingham-52598/.

Angie Martoccio, "Stevie Nicks: I Believe in the Church of Stevie," *Rolling Stone,* October 24, 2024.

Christopher Connelly, "The Second Life of Don Henley," *GQ,* August 1991.

Melanie Davis, "Don Henley Thought Stevie Nicks Wrote This Track for Him, She Says 'He Wishes,'" *American Songwriter,* August 19, 2024, americansongwriter.com/don-henley-thought-stevie-nicks-wrote-this-track-for-him-she-says-he-wishes/.

Steve Pond, "The *US* Interview: Stevie Nicks," *US* magazine, July 9–23, 1990, rockalittle.com/us1.htm.

Andrew Means, "A Wild Heart," *Arizona Republic,* September 18, 1983, stevienicks.info/1983/09/18/a-wild-heart-stevie-nicks/.

"Behind the Music: Stevie Nicks," VH1, November 1, 1998, https://archive.org/details/vh1behindthemusicnovember11998stevienicks convertvideoonline.com.

Stephen Davis, *Gold Dust Woman: The Biography of Stevie Nicks* (St. Martin's Press, 2017).

Emily Weaver, "Stevie Nicks' Dating History: From Lindsey Buckingham to Joe Walsh," *People* magazine, September 11, 2023, people.com/stevie-nicks-complete-dating-history-7502107.

Timespace: The Best of Stevie Nicks liner notes (1991).

Mick Brown, "Stevie Nicks: A Survivor's Story," *The Telegraph,* September 8, 2007, https://www.telegraph.co.uk/culture/3667803/Stevie-Nicks-a-survivors-story.html.

"My Life in Pictures," *People* magazine, May 4, 2009, https://stevienicks.info/2009/05/04/stevie-nicks-my-life-in-pictures/.

Sheryl Crow, "With Her First Solo Album in Seven Years, Rock's Poetess Finds Her Life Is Rhyming Once Again," *Interview* magazine, May 2001, https://www.fleetwoodmac-uk.com/articles/archive/SNart010.html.

Jancee Dunn, "Women in Rock 2002: Stevie Nicks, at 54, Is Still the Coolest Chick in the Room," *Rolling Stone,* October 31, 2002.

"20 Questions: Stevie Nicks," *Playboy*, July 1982 (Vol. 29, No. 7), http://rockalittle.com/playboy1.htm.

Stevie Nicks: Through the Looking Glass, documentary film, directed by Elio España (2013).

Jenny Stevens, "Stevie Nicks on Art, Ageing and Attraction: 'Botox Makes It Look Like You're in a Satanic Cult!,'" *The Guardian,* October 14, 2020.

Lesson Eleven: Never Stop Being a Romantic

"20 Questions: Stevie Nicks," *Playboy,* July 1982 (Vol. 29, No. 7), http://rockalittle.com/playboy1.htm.

Amy Kaufman, "The Moonlight Confessions of Stevie Nicks," *Los Angeles Times,* September 30, 2020.

"Stevie Nicks on the Importance of Being a Romantic," *Creative Independent,* October 22, 2016, fleetwoodmacnews.com/2016/10/interview-stevie-nicks-on-importance-of.html.

Stephen Davis, *Gold Dust Woman: The Biography of Stevie Nicks* (St. Martin's Press, 2017).

Oprah's Master Class, OWN (2013).

Tusk liner notes (1979).

Tommy Vance Show, May 1994.

Leah Greenblatt, "Stevie Nicks On Her Favorite Songs: A Music Mix Exclusive," *Entertainment Weekly,* March 31, 2009, ew.com/article/2009/03/31/stevie-nicks-in/.

Morgan Enos, "Stevie Nicks' 10 Best Songs," *Billboard* magazine, March 26, 2019, billboard.com/music/rock/stevie-nicks-10-best-songs-hits-8503602/.

Spinner.com (2011), thefalconsnest.wordpress.com/2011/04/26/stevie-nicks-secret-love-2/.

Lesson Twelve: Don't Be Afraid of Changing

Caroline Sullivan, "The Witch Is Back," *The Guardian,* February 12, 1998, rockalittle.com/guardian1.htm.

Rapido! featuring Stevie Nicks, Paul McCartney, Sam Kinison, and Jon Bon Jovi (YouTube, 1988), youtube.com/watch?v=dr8vgrLlKnw.

Blair Jackson, "Stevie: Fleetwood Mac's Siren Soars with Her First Solo Album, Bella Donna," *BAM* magazine, September 11, 1981.
Timothy White, "Stevie Nicks' Magic Act," *Rolling Stone,* September 3, 1981.
Stevie Nicks: Through the Looking Glass (2013).
The Wild Heart liner notes (1983).
Mark Goodman, "Stevie: Wild Angel on the Wing," Faces Interview of the Month, MTV (1983).
Stephen Davis, *Gold Dust Woman: The Biography of Stevie Nicks* (St. Martin's Press, 2017).
Fred Schruers, "Fleetwood Mac: Back on the Chain Gang," *Rolling Stone,* October 30, 1997, rollingstone.com/music/music-news/fleetwood-mac-back-on-the-chain-gang-243176/.
Andy Greene, "Fleetwood Mac Detail New Tour and Talk Life After Lindsey Buckingham," *Rolling Stone,* April 25, 2018, rollingstone.com/music/music-features/fleetwood-mac-detail-new-tour-and-talk-life-after-lindsey-buckingham-630624/.
Codie Bullen, "Fleetwood Mac in Talks for Huge Reunion for 50th Anniversary of Classic Album—as Stevie Nicks and Lindsey Buckingham Are 'on a Healing Journey' After Decades-Long Feud," *Daily Mail,* October 21, 2025, dailymail.co.uk/tvshowbiz/article-15214125/Fleetwood-Mac-huge-reunion-50th-anniversary-feud.html.

Lesson Thirteen: Only You Can Save Yourself

Jon Wiederhorn, "After Battling Drug Addiction and Writer's Block, Stevie Nicks Finds Her Shangri-La," CDNow.com, rockalittle.com/.
Oprah's Master Class, OWN (2013).
Brian Hiatt, "Stevie Nicks: A Rock Goddess Looks Back," *Rolling Stone,* January 29, 2015.
Peter Herbst, "Fleetwood Mac Not Hurt by Stevie Nicks," *Rolling Stone,* August 24, 1977, rollingstone.com/music/music-news/fleetwood-mac-not-hurt-by-stevie-nicks-199673/.
Angie Martoccio, "Stevie Nicks: I Believe in the Church of Stevie," *Rolling Stone,* October 24, 2024, rollingstone.com/music/music-features/stevie-nicks-fleetwood-mac-kamala-harris-new-music-1235140437/.
Craig Marks and Rob Tannenbaum, *I Want My MTV: The Uncensored Story of the Music Video Revolution* (Plume, 2012).
Stephen Davis, *Gold Dust Woman: The Biography of Stevie Nicks* (St. Martin's Press, 2017).
Michael Martin, "Edge of Everything: The Inevitable Return of Stevie

Nicks," *Out* magazine, September 11, 2014, out.com/entertainment/music/2014/09/11/inevitable-return-stevie-nicks.
John Kordosh, "Fleetwood Mac Return Without Leaving," *Creem* magazine, September 1, 1987.
Rob Sheffield, "How Stevie Nicks' Lost Masterpiece 'Ooh My Love' Became a Cult Fan Favorite," *Rolling Stone,* May 30, 2019, rollingstone.com/music/music-features/steve-nicks-ooh-my-love-rob-sheffield-841005/.
Jenny Stevens, "Stevie Nicks on Art, Ageing and Attraction: 'Botox Makes It Look Like You're in a Satanic Cult!,'" *The Guardian,* October 14, 2020.
The Chris Isaak Hour (2009), youtube.com/watch?v=-1IzkcW22JA, youtube.com/watch?v=h93pGqpq5jo, youtube.com/watch?v=pCgJszwSFQo.
Chrissy Iley, "Joe Walsh and I Were Doing So Much Cocaine We Were Sure We Were Going to Die," Living Scotsman.com, September 30, 2007, fleetwoodmacnews.com/2007/09/.
Behind the Music, VH1 (1998).
ABC Downtown Interview (2001), https://www.youtube.com/watch?v=MjzDQxpCTRc.
Fleetwood Mac: Don't Stop, BBC (2009), youtube.com/watch?v=FJrT5OUrew4.
60 Minutes Australia (2017), youtube.com/watch?v=NaWU2YisjFk.
Gia Kourlas, "Sobriety Test: After Kicking Pills and Overcoming Writer's Block, Stevie Nicks Comes Clean on Her New Album," *Time Out New York,* issue 292, April 26–May 3, 2001, rockalittle.com/interview_time_out_ny_apr2001.htm.
Jerry Gladstone, "Stevie Shares Lessons Learned from Battling Drugs, Her Own Ego," *Arts Management Magazine (AMM),* December 2020, stevienicks.info/2020/12/19/amm-inspiration-with-stevie-nicks/.

Lesson Fourteen: Don't Let Them Take Your Power

Stevie Nicks Official Instagram (2024).
Stephen Davis, *Gold Dust Woman: The Biography of Stevie Nicks* (St. Martin's Press, 2017).
Amber Raiken, "Stevie Nicks Shares Regret over Not Voting Until She Was 70," *The Independent,* October 31, 2024, the-independent.com/arts-entertainment/music/news/stevie-nicks-presidential-endorsement-vote-harris-b2639123.html.
Zoë Howe, *Stevie Nicks: Visions, Dreams, and Rumours* (Omnibus Press, 2015).

"Stevie's Journal Entries Regarding Visits to the Injured Troops," *The Nicks Fix,* January 14, 2006, rockalittle.com/journal_visiting_troops.htm.
Timespace: The Best of Stevie Nicks liner notes (1991).
"Stevie Nicks: Soldier's Angel," *People* magazine (2011).
Stevie Nicks: In Your Dreams, documentary film (2013).
Angie Martoccio, "Stevie Nicks: I Believe in the Church of Stevie," *Rolling Stone,* October 24, 2024.
"SXSW interview: Stevie Nicks," March 14, 2013, stevienicks.info/2013/03/14/sxsw-interview-stevie-nicks/.
Tracy Smith, "Stevie Nicks on 'The Lighthouse,' Her Rallying Cry for Women's Rights," CBS News, October 27, 2024, cbsnews.com/news/stevie-nicks-on-the-lighthouse-her-rallying-cry-for-womens-rights/.
Chloe Melas, "Stevie Nicks Reveals Fleetwood Mac's 'Paid the Same' Policy," CNN.com, January 27, 2018, edition.cnn.com/2018/01/27/entertainment/stevie-nicks-pay-equity/index.html.

Lesson Fifteen: Don't Have Rivals. Have Friends

Tavi Gevinson, "Stevie Nicks Is Still Living Her Dreams," *New Yorker,* February 15, 2022, newyorker.com/culture/the-new-yorker-interview/stevie-nicks-tavi-gevinson-conversation.
Andy Greene, "Christine McVie on Navigating the 'Storm' of Fleetwood Mac and the Genius of Peter Green," *Rolling Stone,* June 23, 2022.
Sean Egan, *Fleetwood Mac on Fleetwood Mac: Interviews and Encounters* (Chicago Review Press, 2016).
Tim Jonze, "Fleetwood Mac's Stevie and Christine: 'We Were Like Rock'n'roll Nuns,'" *The Guardian,* December 12, 2013, theguardian.com/music/2013/dec/12/fleetwood-mac-stevie-nicks-christine-mcvie-nuns.
Nigel Williamson, "Fleetwood Mac: 'Everybody Was Pretty Weirded Out'—the Story of Rumours," *Uncut* magazine, May 2003.
Stephen Davis, *Gold Dust Woman: The Biography of Stevie Nicks* (St. Martin's Press, 2017).
Jim Ladd, "Fleetwood Mac—Tusk Interview" (1979), inherownwords.com/witches.htm.
Angie Martoccio, "Stevie Nicks: I Believe in the Church of Stevie," *Rolling Stone,* October 24, 2024.
Zoë Howe, *Stevie Nicks: Visions, Dreams, and Rumours* (Omnibus Press, 2015).
Paul Zollo and Tom Petty, *Conversations with Tom Petty* (Omnibus Press, 2005).
Stevie Nicks: In Your Dreams, documentary film (2013).

Blair Jackson, "Stevie: Fleetwood Mac's Siren Soars with Her First Solo Album, Bella Donna," *BAM* magazine, September 11, 1981.
Modern Records, *Stevie Nicks: The Wild Heart,* press release (1983), stevienicks.info/music/stevie-nicks-the-wild-heart-1983/i-will-run-to-you-with-tom-petty-the-heartbreakers/.
Kara Manning, *Rolling Stone* review (1994).
Entertainment Tonight archive, obituary for Dallas Taylor (1990), youtube.com/watch?v=wIRxwYKpPDk.
Street Angel liner notes (1994).
Kelly Murphy, "How Tom Petty Encouraged Stevie Nicks to Work Again After a 'Terrible Record,'" *Far Out* magazine, June 7, 2024, faroutmagazine.co.uk/tom-petty-encouraged-stevie-nicks-to-work-again/.
"Stevie Nicks Comments on 'Don't Come Around Here No More,'" VH1, youtube.com/watch?v=_QL8L5RGn2E.
"In My Dreams and In Your Dreams by Stevie Nicks," ABC Music Lounge, May 20, 2011, fleetwoodmacnews.com/2011/05/stevie-nicks-from-beginning.html.
Rob Sheffield, "Stevie Nicks on Twirling, Kicking Drugs and a Lifetime with Lindsey," *Rolling Stone,* October 2, 2014.
Ethan Millman, "Harry Styles, Stevie Nicks Duet 'Landslide' in Emotional Tribute to Christine McVie," *Rolling Stone,* July 12, 2024, rollingstone.com/music/music-news/harry-styles-stevie-nicks-christine-mcvie-tribute-landslide-1235059599/.
Amy Kaufman, "The Moonlight Confessions of Stevie Nicks," *Los Angeles Times,* September 30, 2020.

Lesson Sixteen: Be a Teacher

Robert Burke Warren, "Me & Stevie Nicks," Showfolk, May 4, 2025 (interview originally conducted in 2011), robertburkewarren.substack.com/p/me-and-stevie-nicks.
Oprah's Master Class, OWN (2013).
Rob Tannenbaum, "Stevie's Secret History," *Billboard* magazine, October 4, 2014 (Vol. 126, No. 32), stevienicks.info/2014/10/04/stevies-secret-history/.
"The Making of *Rumours,*" VH1 (1997).
In the Studio with Fleetwood Mac, www3.rocktrop (year unknown, likely ca. 1997), inherownwords.com/dreams.htm.

Lesson Seventeen: You Can Borrow from Me Anytime

Larry Flick, "Stevie Nicks Returns with Sheryl Crow in Tow," *Billboard* magazine, February 12, 2001.

Jessica Goodman, "How Stevie Nicks Created a Coven of Gold Dust Women," *Huffington Post,* December 3, 2014, stevienicks.info/2014/12/03/how-stevie-nicks-created-a-coven-of-gold-dust-women/.

David Wild, "Q&A: Stevie Nicks," *Rolling Stone,* July 5, 2001, rollingstone.com/music/music-news/qa-stevie-nicks-49947/.

Los Angeles Times, August 16, 2001.

Katherine J. Igoe, "At 28, Sheryl Crow Was Waiting Tables and Mingling with Music Legends," *Bustle,* August 14, 2021, bustle.com/entertainment/sheryl-crow-stevie-nicks-music-indstury-sexism-quotes.

Brian Hiatt, "Taylor Swift in Wonderland," *Rolling Stone,* October 25, 2012, rollingstone.com/music/music-news/taylor-swift-in-wonderland-180107/.

Stevie Nicks, "Taylor Swift," *Time* magazine 100 Most Influential (April 2010), fleetwoodmacnews.com/2010/04/taylor-swift-by-stevie-nicks-time.html.

Today show (Australia), "Taylor Swift Talks About Stevie Nicks" (February 2010), youtube.com/watch?v=SouFjEOe51M.

"Stevie Nicks Reacts to Taylor Swift's Tribute to Her During Dublin Eras Show," *Entertainment Tonight,* July 1, 2024, youtube.com/watch?v=eyAn-TL0Yz4.

Tavi Gevinson, "Stevie Nicks Is Still Living Her Dreams," *New Yorker,* February 15, 2022.

Express (UK), December 1, 2014, https://stevienicks.info/2014/12/01/stevie-haim-are-major-force-in-rock-and-roll/.

"Miley Cyrus Got the Coolest Letter from Stevie Nicks," *The Tonight Show Starring Jimmy Fallon,* September 10, 2020, youtube.com/watch?v=i5OVtyvXpck.

"Miley Cyrus 'Edge of Midnight' on the Stern Show," *The Howard Stern Show,* December 4, 2020, youtube.com/watch?v=YGY5Z58PRMs.

Brittany Spanos and Amy X. Wang, "Read Harry Styles' Heartwarming Rock Hall Tribute to Stevie Nicks," *Rolling Stone,* March 29, 2019, rollingstone.com/music/music-news/harry-styles-stevie-nicks-rock-and-roll-hall-of-fame-2019-813901/.

Jenny Stevens, "Stevie Nicks on Art, Ageing and Attraction: 'Botox Makes It Look Like You're in a Satanic Cult!,'" *The Guardian,* October 14, 2020.

About the Author

RACHEL BRODSKY is a music and culture writer. She has worked for publications including *Stereogum*, *SPIN*, *Paste*, MTV.com, Grammy.com, and *The Independent*. Her writing has also been published in *Rolling Stone*, *TIME*, *Los Angeles Times*, *The Ringer*, *Nylon*, *Bustle*, *The Guardian*, *GQ*, *Vulture*, and others. She currently lives in Los Angeles.